MORE GOD, MOTORCYCLES, AND OPEN ROADS

ENDORSEMENTS

An exceptional book of truth-telling and hope. Tim is a fine wide-open-spaces and wide-open-heart writer. This volume of stories does not fail to inspire and bless the reader to their core. I cannot recommend it enough. A long bright road of stars.
—**Murray Pura**, author *Grace Rider*

Although not a biker myself, as a sports car guy, I find we tend to love the same roads for the same reasons. As a follower of Jesus Christ, I find Tim's devos reach me at the deepest levels.
—**E. Wayne Kempton**, author, pastor, federal special agent. Mazda Miata

Here is your spiritual field guide for before, during, after or planning your next road trip adventure!
—**Toby Erickson**, author, educator. Suzuki VSTROM DL1000

Tim has been a friend for several years and piqued my interest in riding. I bought my first bike in my mid-60s and sold it a few years later due to age concerns. My most memorable ride was a day long trip with Tim ... a ride we only talk about in code. More than a biker buddy, Tim has challenged and encouraged my spiritual walk. We continue to meet monthly and I highly recommend anything he writes.

—**Greg England**, pastor. Suzuki Boulevard

I once rode a Honda 50, and I once rode on the back of Tim's bike coming down the steep mountain grade on the Bishop Creek Road. That taught me to stick to hiking. His Gray Hogs are all my friends.

If you like adventure, if you like good descriptions of adventurous trips, if you like experiences of men doing wild things, *More God, Motorcycles, and Open Roads*, by Tim Riter is for you. Once again, I am happy and proud to recommend this book to you, as I did for the first *God, A Motorcycle, and The Open Road*. You will enjoy this book and go to school on the earthy wisdom. This book would make a great Christmas gift for your adventure friends. Lots of laughs and good dreams of future journeys ahead!

—**Dr. James Price,** pastor, educator

This unique devotional effortlessly shifts from the open road to an open Bible. Readers will rev up their spiritual lives and kick-start their faith with this joyful, fun, yet thoughtful book. Author Tim Riter (and several guest contributors) weaves biker stories with helpful counsel, unexpected life lessons, humorous stories, inspiring admonitions, and encouraging truth. His love of nature, travel, God, and of course, motorcycles, shines through on every page.

Keri Wyatt Kent, coauthor of *Live Like a Guide Dog* and 25 other books

"Ride majestically! Ride triumphantly!" Those sentences are from the Psalms, but Tim Riter treats them as more than metaphorical. His devotional combines the thrill of riding motorcycles with the joy of living for the Lord. His book captures the energy of the Christian life in a winning, memorable way.

—**Joseph Bentz,** author of *Nothing is Wasted,* educator

Tim Riter loves adventure, particularly via a motorcycle on an open road. More importantly, he loves the Lord, and on these rides around our beautiful country he shares with his readers devotional insights that end with encouragement, and sometimes challenges both of which cause this reader to grow spiritually. Do yourself a favor and ride along with Tim from the comfort of your favorite chair!

—**Leilani Strong Smith**, author, educator

I was grateful to help Tim Riter's first biker devo ride its way into publication, and I am delighted to recommend this continuation of the journey. Tim and some road-worthy friends explore the natural connections between journeys on the open road with the journeys of faith.

—**Todd Hafer**, author, editor. Kawasaki 250 dirt bike ("lovingly" retired by his wife prior to first wedding anniversary)

From training and pruning an apple tree to Iron Butt rides, Tim has captured exceptional life and faith object lessons for all those who ride. And for those who don't ride, who used to, or who someday want to, the lure of nature's beauty experienced from two wheels is both refreshing and exhilarating. Reading Tim's words is a great way to begin your day.

—**Libby Taylor**, author

People look for God in different places—in a beautiful sunset, in a restless ocean, or in church on Sunday morning. Tim Riter finds God while riding on his motorcycle. His new book is not so much a devotional as it is an adventure—the adventure believers can fall into when they keep their heart and mind open to the things God reveals in the world

around them. It is also a book for those who have not come to a saving faith in Christ, for Tim points out in every chapter what we of faith already know—the heavens (and the earth) declare the glory of God. A book for everyone.
—**Patrick E. Craig,** six-time CIBA award winner, Selah Award winner, and Word Guild of Canada Award Winner

Author Tim Riter offers the kind of wisdom that's learned from making wrong turns, weathering storms, and discovering beauty both on the mountains and in the valleys. *More God, Motorcycles, and Open Roads* upshifts your alone time with God to the next gear by provoking thought rather than offering trite answers. The stories are entertaining and the messages relatable for those who grip freedom by the handlebars.
—**Angela Ruth Strong**, author of *Fiancé Finale*. The backseat of an Indian Pursuit

TIM RITER
MORE GOD, MOTORCYCLES, AND OPEN ROADS

A Christian Company
ElkLakePublishingInc.com

COPYRIGHT NOTICE

More God, Motorcycles, and Open Roads

First edition. Copyright © 2024 by Tim Riter. The information contained in this book is the intellectual property of Tim Riter and is governed by United States and International copyright laws. All rights reserved. No part of this publication, either text or image, may be used for any purpose other than personal use. Therefore, reproduction, modification, storage in a retrieval system, or retransmission, in any form or by any means, electronic, mechanical, or otherwise, for reasons other than personal use, except for brief quotations for reviews or articles and promotions, is strictly prohibited without prior written permission by the publisher.

NO AI TRAINING: Without in any way limiting Tim Riter's and publisher's exclusive rights under copyright, any use of this publication to "train" generative artificial intelligence (AI) technologies to generate text is expressly prohibited. The author reserves all rights to license uses of this work for generative AI training and development of machine learning language models.

Unless otherwise noted, all scriptures are from THE HOLY BIBLE, NEW INTERNATIONAL VERSION®. Copyright© 1973, 1978, 1984, 2011 by Biblica, Inc.™. Used by permission of Zondervan.

Scripture quotations marked (NLT) are taken from the *Holy Bible*, New Living Translation, copyright ©1996, 2004, 2015 by Tyndale House Foundation. Used by permission of Tyndale House Publishers, Carol Stream, Illinois 60188. All rights reserved.

Scripture quotations marked MSG are taken from *The Message*, copyright © 1993, 2002, 2018 by Eugene H. Peterson. Used by permission of NavPress. All rights reserved. Represented by Tyndale House Publishers. CONTEMPORARY ENGLISH (TM): Scripture taken from THE MESSAGE: THE BIBLE IN CONTEMPORARY ENGLISH, copyright©1993, 1994, 1995, 1996, 2000, 2001, 2002. Used by permission of NavPress Publishing Group.

All Greek and Hebrew word translations were taken from the Strong's Concordance section of *The Online Bible*.

Italics in quoted Scriptures indicate emphasis added by the author.

MORE GOD, MOTORCYCLES, AND OPEN ROAD | ix

Cover and Interior Design: Kelly Artieri, Deb Haggerty

Editor(s): Kristin Cooney, Judy Hagey, Deb Haggerty

Author Represented By: AuthorizeMe Literary Firm LLC

PUBLISHED BY: Elk Lake Publishing, Inc., 35 Dogwood Drive, Plymouth, MA 02360, 2024

Library Cataloging Data

Names: Riter, Tim / Tim Riter

More God, Motorcycles, and Open Roads / Tim Riter

186 p. 23cm × 15cm (9in × 6 in.)

ISBN-13: 9798891342958 (paperback) | 9798891342965 (trade paperback) | 9798891342972 (e-book)

Key Words: Christian Men's Issues; Traveler and Explorer Biographies; Christian Devotionals; Adventure Stories; Motorcycle Stories; Travelogues and Travel Essays; Christian Personal Growth

Library of Congress Control Number: 2024948147 Nonfiction

DEDICATION

Like my first devotional, *God, a Motorcycle, and the Open Road*, this sequel, *More God, Motorcycles, and Open Roads*, is dedicated to all the riders who led the way, who taught me to thrive and survive on two wheels.

My dad, Lynn Riter, first delivered telegrams in Los Angeles on a belt-drive Excelsior bike, later rode an Indian, and set a world record in the Cannonball cross-country run in a Ford Model A. I suspect he passed on to me the drive to challenge myself.

The Gray Hogs, our regular riding crew of Jerry, Mick, Brad, and Rich, have shared a lot of miles and smiles over a lot of years. Thanks for the rich rides, my friends, and I'll miss the adventures we've shared. Larry Clark built my second bike, a semi-chopped custom '73 Honda CB 750. I still remember, use, and pass on his tips.

And my wife, Sheila, who took a lot of rides, including some long ones. In one hot desert stretch, she mopped my head and neck with cool water to keep us alive. Though she can't ride now, she graciously supports my continued insanity of riding.

Most of all, to God, who has gifted us with not only grace but also a beautiful creation, one with enough order that motorcycles can be designed!

TABLE OF CONTENTS

Dedication xi
Acknowledgments xv
1—Getting Into It 1
2—Born to Be Wild 5
3—Of Mountains and Miniatures 9
4—No Good Deed Goes Unpunished 13
5—Challenge Yourself 17
6—Find Your limits 21
7—Unexpected Provision 25
8—Dodging Obstacles 31
9—To Cruise or Not to Cruise 35
10—See the Big Picture 39
11—Seasons 43
12—Serenity or Stress 47
13—Ruby and Me 51
14—When Biking Isn't Enough 55
15—Strange Destinations 59
16—Start Hard 63
17—70 Isn't 28 67
18—No Longer an Outsider 71
19—Balancing Risks 75
20—Try Some Road Kindness 79
21—Patience Pays Off 83
22—Variety & Differences 87

23—Life Lessons 91
24—Offer Help 95
25—Seek Help 99
26—You Gave Us 103
27—When Fear Cost Me A Beer 107
28—A Snowy Pass 111
29—Outdo One Another 115
30—A Day in the Life of Bikers 119
31—Follow Your Leaders? 123
32—Our Vast and Varied World 127
33—Fighting Fear Pays Off 131
34—How Easy Got His Groove Back 135
35—Creation Care 139
36—The Taste of Gravel 143
37—Two-Week Trip Takes Six Months 147
38—Will This Ever End 151
39—Longing for Belonging 155
40—Man, Machine, Macadam 159
A Note from the Author 163
About the Author 165
Endnotes 167

ACKNOWLEDGMENTS

No author produces a book alone, so thanks are due those who have contributed to getting this book completed. So, great thanks to my agent, Sharon Elliott of AuthorizeMe Now Literary, who not only "got" my writing and goals but also got Deb Haggerty at Elk Lake to take a look at a bit of an unusual book. Muchas gracias, Deb! And kudos to Judy Hagey, who shepherded the project at Elk Lake, and many thanks to Kristin Cooney, a fine editor who improved the book.

And I gratefully appreciate the fine riders and writers who have contributed chapters to this book: Murray Pura, Cherie Dena, Libby Worden, Dan DeWitt, Toby Erickson, Jerry Christensen, Pam Schmoll, Jim Davis, and Deb Terasaki. You have improved the book!

Most importantly, thanks to my patient wife, who put up with me as I ignored some outdoor tasks while writing the book in my study.

May all of this work touch each of you readers, as you discover how God embeds every part of life, not just motorcycling.

1—GETTING INTO IT

"Ride majestically! Ride triumphantly!
Ride on the side of truth!
Ride for the righteous meek!"
—Psalm 45:3–4 (MSG)

Bikes captivate us. The fears we face and still ride. The companionship we develop. The fresh country we'd never experience except for them. The clichéd but true freedom of the open road. The immersion in God's world, unprotected by a steel-and-glass cage. The changes they lead us to. The time to ponder God and our lives and to see his glory and how we can bring him more.

But for years, I never thought of them. I never desired to hop on one until in the summer before my senior year in college, a neighbor almost forced me to try his kids' Honda Trail 90. Just to shut him up, I did. Nice. Not captivating. But nice.

Then, near the end of my senior year, my college roommate and I planned on taking my 1964 Ford Falcon to Canada to visit another friend who had moved there—but things began to change. Mark turned out to not have the money for the trip, and a lady ran into my Falcon on a Los Angeles freeway. I didn't feel confident driving it that far, and the trip evaporated.

During finals week, several of us got tired of studying and headed for a local theater to see *Easy Rider*, the iconic cult film depicting sex, drugs, and bikes. I was entranced. Not with the sex and drugs, although I certainly wasn't walking with Jesus then. But Peter Fonda and Dennis Hopper captured a freedom of traveling on two wheels that captivated me.

The idea burst upon me like inspiration—I'd work for a month or so, save enough to buy a bike and travel costs, and head to Canada for a month before grad school started.

My life has never been the same. I bought a 1970 Honda 350 Scrambler, a cross between a road and dirt bike. Much too small for such a trip. Much too multipurpose for a long tour. Three weeks after the purchase, I took off. Much too soon for a rookie rider. I did make it back for the start of grad school, but more importantly, I graduated into motorcycling. I discovered how a motorcycle could lead to a miracle of a new life.

That first little ride on the Honda 90 pleased me. *Easy Rider* intrigued me. But my first motorcycle long-distance trip transformed me.

Since then, I've driven over 270,000 miles on two wheels. I really can't count my number of multistate trips, but it's in the dozens. One alone covered 31 states and 13,000 miles. I've ridden in all 50 states, the District of Columbia, and three nations. I've changed a flat tire in 110-degree heat, and on the side of a narrow Canadian road, I unjammed a chain that slipped off the sprocket and locked the rear wheel. Returning from a ride to Colorado, I had a main fuse blow, causing my bike to stall on a Los Angeles freeway during rush hour. I eased my way to the side, fixed it, and rode on.

I've got grease under my fingernails and a lot of miles on my butt. I've qualified twice for the Iron Butt Club, limited to those who ride 1,000 miles on two wheels within 24 hours. One at the age of 70.

I know a bit about riding and have learned the close connection riding has with faith for me and many others. Faith my tires will hold their grip on a wet road. Faith the room I reserved for the end of a rainy day will be there. Faith my riding buddies will make the trip better, not worse. Mostly, I've seen how motorcycling has enriched my faith in God, and how faith has enriched my motorcycling.

I began following Jesus at eleven, until the shallowness of my faith led to four years of questioning and searching in college. Ironically, that first Canada trip played a key role in me coming back to God. I've been with him ever since. I've pastored churches and written books about living as a Jesus follower.

This book stands as a sequel to *God, a Motorcycle, and the Open Road* that came out April 1, 2019. Both combine stories, thoughts, meditations, and questions about the intersection of these two passions, following Jesus and biking. Devotions? Yes, but a bit more. Not so much affirming as challenging. They will challenge you to blend Jesus in your life as well, whether or not you ride. The chapters may contain questions that cause you to think of riding—or Christianity—in a new light.

Use them as best fits you. If you're in a group, you may choose to read one at a meeting and kick it around a bit. Or if you're on a ride, start the day with one. Give the book away to fellow riders who may not yet know Jesus. This book is not an evangelistic tract, but it might help them see Jesus in a fresh way. And as you read, you'll notice some chapters are written by other fellow riders, friends who have fine stories to tell.

The stand-alone chapters are not in any particular order, and you might find some stories repeated to give the context. The repetition is intended.

And let me know if this book works for you.

Kick-Starting the Application

What's your experience with bikes? Never ridden? A seasoned biker with calluses on your butt and grease under your fingernails? Rode, but a long time ago? Thinking about getting into riding? What intrigues you about bikes? What about them makes you uneasy?

Whatever your background, I'm glad you hopped on for the ride. I hope you enjoy the stories and are touched by the applications.

2—BORN TO BE WILD

By Murray Pura, AUTHOR, PASTOR, POET, BIKER

A friendly inn and restaurant was off the Island Highway on Vancouver Island, a large island just north of Seattle cheerfully afloat on the Pacific Ocean. Family and friends often went to the Island Inn and Pub to relax and enjoy a good meal. My wife and I were surprised one evening to walk in and find our neighbor Skid there—along with his motorcycle club. Skid was his biker name. I suppose his real name was on his driver's license and other legal documents, but other than that, he'd left his birth name so far behind he couldn't even spot it in his rearview mirror. I'd seen a few photos of his earlier life back East—short hair, clean shaven, preppy V-neck sweaters.

Now he wore long hair, a long beard, blue jeans, and black leather. I guess he might have looked intimidating to those who didn't know him. But he was a friendly neighbor to my wife and me, full of smiles and laughter. We often talked about God and Jesus. We had amicable talks that harbored no ill will or bad tempers. So, it was easy to walk over to Skid's table and greet his girlfriend along with the dozen or so rough-looking members of his biker club.

The round of handshakes came off so easily, an idea began to form in my head. As my wife and I dug into our burgers and fries, the idea took shape and firmed up. When the stage opened for karaoke, I immediately got to my feet, took the mic, asked the DJ for the song I'd selected, then called to Skid. "Come on up. We're going to do 'Born to be Wild.' Sing it with me."

Skid's eyes went huge. "What? Me? Sing here? No way!"

"C'mon, Skid, it's the iconic biker song. Jump up, and we'll sing it together."

"No way, man, no way!"

"Okay, well, I'm going to sing it, and I'm dedicating it to you and your biker friends." So the DJ rolled out the song, and I began to sing out the lyrics on the screen. I went through the first verse and the chorus. I was just heading into the second verse when I spotted Skid off my right shoulder belting it out. A quick glance showed five or six of the biker club grouped together and getting into the song with Skid and me.

By the time we'd reached the second chorus, the whole club was up there, surrounding me and Skid, filling the stage, and singing the song at the top of their lungs. We roared out the tune to a grand finale, laughing and hugging as we brought it to an end. We had a great time.

But little did we know we'd been photographed. And for years afterward, a framed copy of the picture hung on the wall of the Island Inn and Pub. When people asked about this picture of a tough-looking biker gang in leather and boots surrounding a tall man in a white T-shirt and jeans, they were told, "Oh, that's just the local biker club hanging out with their pastor."

Murray's story touches my heart because the movie *Easy Rider* featured that song, and that movie changed the trajectory of my life. I now start off every long road trip singing "Born to be Wild." But the song itself and Murray's story transcend biking with a message of freedom and power for all followers of Jesus.

Truly, we are born to be wild but are not meant to match one of the definitions of the word from *Merriam-Webster*: "uncivilized, barbaric." Although this definition may be a common connotation of *wild*, *Merriam* also includes two others: "going beyond normal or conventional bounds" and "deviating from the intended or expected course."[1]

We all face restrictions based on others' expectations and society's desires plus our own flaws and brokenness. We need to realize God crafted us to be wild, to embrace the world and transcend unbiblical limits. We are meant to follow his leading, as Jesus told us about in John 10:10: "I have come that they may have life, and have it to the full." Let's explore some ways we can blast through mediocre lives.

Birds of a feather flock together, right? So, we create affinity groups, such as ones for bikers, radio-controlled airplane groups, or churches. We go where we're comfortable and fit in, only to become a holy huddle, rarely interacting with those different from us. Our reluctance to reach beyond our comfort zone is why the pic on the wall of the Island Inn and Pub, a tall man with a white T-shirt surrounded by leather-clad bikers, is so cool. Murray took the initiative to reach outside his comfort zone by singing a nonchurch biker song, and the bikers responded when they saw their similarities. They all broke through their boundaries for a positive spiritual impact. The bikers received a pastor from the song.

Paul got that process: "When I was with the Jews, I lived like a Jew to bring the Jews to Christ … When I am with the Gentiles who do not follow the Jewish law, I too live apart from that law so I can bring them to Christ … Yes, I try to find *common ground with everyone*, doing everything I can to save some" (1 Corinthians 9:20–22 NLT).

We tend to avoid those who differ from us, maybe out of fear, discomfort, or not knowing how to approach them. Perhaps we need to intentionally find some common ground and break free from conventional bounds.

Think about our major life choices. Others expect—or require—us to do what they desire, parents especially. My dad's boss's son brought in bank as an insurance actuary, and because I did well with math, he pushed me in that direction. I knew that career would bore me, but Dad had a hard time accepting my decision.

Others expect us to live conventionally, and their expectations can bind us. Maybe we need to blast into freedom. Not the freedom to be "uncivilized and barbaric," but to be the person God designed us to be. To be unconventional. To match not just our talents but our personality and experiences.

Kick-Starting the Application

Have you felt bound by others' expectations? By society? By your flaws and failures? Do you sense God has something better in store for you? Are you willing to blast through all of these pressures with God's help?

Murray Pura, who holds both Master of Divinity and Master of Theology degrees, has been on the mission field and served on several churches' pastoral teams. A prolific author, he has published novels and inspirational books with Elk Lake, Baker, Barbour, Harvest House, Zondervan, and HarperCollins. Murray lives in southwestern Alberta, Canada. You can visit his website at www.murrayandrewpura.com.

3—OF MOUNTAINS AND MINIATURES

A few years back, the Gray Hogs headed for Banff to snag Mick's bucket list of figuring out why that town has such a big reputation. Jerry and I did a separate pre-trip ride to Wisconsin and met Mick and Brad in Shelby, Montana, intending to head north and skirt Calgary to approach Banff from the east. But while checking out of the hotel in Shelby, we met a fellow biker who told us of a rustic but inexpensive motel in Radium Hot Springs. We decided to change our route, which bikers seem to do a lot.

We crossed the Canadian border just north of Shelby and took several circuitous and gorgeous roads to Radium Hot Springs. The hotel lived up to the recommendation (if you'd like to see the pics, you can email me). The motel keeper even took us to the hot springs in her car so we wouldn't have to ride back damp. Canadians are truly helpful, and the hot water soothed some aching biker muscles ... more than once.

The next morning's ride to Banff thrilled us, despite the cold. The city was nice, although a bit overdeveloped. We struggled to find a breakfast place, but the one we picked came with marvelous mountain views in all directions.

That brief visit satisfied Mick, and we left Banff headed north to Lake Louise. The lake was quite pretty but overcrowded, so we continued north with numerous stops to take in the stupendous scenery. Believe me, Alberta and British Columbia will strike you with wonder. Then we hit Bow Lake. Awestruck, we stared in silence. Bow Peak guarded the lake from above, a huge stratified mountain bent at a 45-degree angle with no fractures.

God created ongoing processes to lay down the sediment layers and to heat, raise, and bend that massive mountain. What kind of God is this? That mountain, so huge from our human perspective, rises 3,320 feet above Bow Lake's surface. The height is the equivalent of stacking 553 people all six feet tall. I felt humbled just looking at it. And Bow Peak is a miniscule portion of the earth. And this earth is merely a small globe circling a small sun that is one of ten billion trillion. His power and wisdom overwhelm me.

Then, as we walked a short distance south to get a different view, I spotted a delicate multicolored wildflower—created by God with fragile beauty. Any of us could have easily crushed this creation of his, merely by not noticing it as we walked. Could such a misstep verge on blasphemy toward a God who loves beauty so much he imbeds it in a small flower? A flower dwarfed by us humans, who were dwarfed by the mountain, which was dwarfed by our planet, which was ... well, we could go on, but I suspect you get the picture.

As I knelt to take a pic, I almost prostrated myself in worship. Not of the mountain or the flower, but of the vastness of a God who could create both. A God with the power to carve a mountain. With the delicacy to form a tiny wildflower. With the appreciation of beauty he imbedded in us. A beauty with little practical purpose except to give joy to his human creation. And a joy that, too often, too many of us ignore. Who walk by.

Let's explore his creation and our responsibility: "Then God planted a garden in Eden, in the east. He put the Man he had just made in it. God made all kinds of trees grow from the ground, trees beautiful to look at and good to eat" (Genesis 2:8–9 MSG). God designed our world with beauty. Why? I guess a blend of his own beauty and his love of beauty. A grace gift from him. I suspect that beauty makes up one of the reasons I ride: being in the midst of this beauty helps me see the transcendent worth of its Creator. Worship.

But he didn't stop at putting us in a beautiful garden with great food: "The LORD God took the man and put him in the Garden of Eden to *work it* and *take care of it*" (Genesis 2:15). The Lord gave us beauty, food, and a job—to take care of it. The original Hebrew root word in *Strong's Concordance* for "take care of" comes from planting a hedge with thorns to protect it. It's also translated or defined as to guard, attend to, preserve, regard.

Note that God didn't give us ownership of the garden, merely possession. It still belongs to him. And I suspect he expects us to pass it along better than how we received it. Frankly, that makes me shudder some. Okay, a lot. But beauty typically needs care to keep it in its best form. God's job was to give us a fine home with beauty and provision. Motorcycle trips remind me of the job he gave us—to protect and enhance and enjoy his creation.

I can love a gracious God like this. I can serve a trusting God like this. I can craft my life around a beauty-loving God like this. I can do my part to take care of all his creation, both living and nonliving. I hope you can too.

KICK-STARTING THE APPLICATION

What most makes you aware of the attributes of God we've discussed in this chapter? I suspect our methods will differ, but we each need to find our pathway to notice the sacredness of God. What impact does not focusing on the spiritual routes that work for you have on your relationships with people? With God? With sin?

One last question, an unavoidable one. Do you do your part in caring for God's creation? One task we did at Bow Lake was pick up the trash others had left. Others had ignored the trash cans. It just didn't seem right to allow the trash to diminish the beauty God provided for us. And yes, that story arrives in our next chapter.

4—NO GOOD DEED GOES UNPUNISHED

Many consider Lake Louise the jewel of the Banff region in Canada, and it did impress our riding group. The clarity of the glacial water and the massiveness of the surrounding mountains affected us small humans. However, all the humans gathered there for the view created quite a crowd, which somewhat diminished our appreciation of it. So, after a short visit, we headed north to Bow Lake, just 24 miles (or 39 km for our Canadian friends), a view which entranced our Gray Hog group even more. Perhaps the less-than-crowded conditions played a role in our enjoyment—bikers tend to avoid crowds. But the shape of the mountain struck us with wonder, as the previous chapter described.

We took pics of the lake and Crowfoot Mountain from the central area, then strolled south for another angle of the glacier. Out of Canada's many impressive qualities, we noticed the almost total lack of litter, which certainly contributed to the natural beauty.

Until, walking back to our bikes, we stopped for an up-close view of some wildflowers along the road and noticed several dozen pieces of trash where some cars had been parked. The incongruity of such natural marvels and the garbage left by humans embarrassed us. Seeing a trash can

20 meters away (meters up north, or 70 feet for those down south), we began picking up the debris. Brad pointed out something close to me, litter, he thought. But as I bent to pick up the "trash," my closer inspection revealed it as a $20 Canadian bill, about $15 US.

Our good deed benefitted us, or at least me, and made me happy, though I'd have been almost as glad if Brad had grabbed it first. A good deed rewarded!

Then I thought of the popular line "No good deed goes unpunished." While Brad received no punishment, his good deed brought him no personal reward—perhaps I should have shared it with him. But the refrain reflects our skeptical culture—one often with truth behind it. Some of our good deeds do get rewarded; many go unnoticed. Others get punished. So, why do good if two of the three options don't pay us back? This question comes at us on several levels, all of which have significance.

Why do good if it can't get us to heaven? That's a valid question because we can't do enough good to balance our sin: "God saved you by his grace when you believed. And you can't take credit for this; it is a gift from God. Salvation is not a reward for the good things we have done, so none of us can boast about it" (Ephesians 2:8–9 NLT).

Why do good if it can't guarantee good results? I suspect we'd all agree the apostles did a lot of good acts, but all but one ended up being killed for their faith. Hmmm.

Why do good if it causes people to view us as soft and take advantage of us?

Why do good?

We choose good because it matches our salvation destiny: "For we are God's masterpiece. He has created us anew in Christ Jesus, so we can *do the good things* he planned for us long ago" (Ephesians 2:10 NLT). We do good not to get into a relationship with God but because we first connect with him. Good stuff works well as a result of faith but fails as a cause of faith.

We choose good because it allows us to reflect God's nature. This next verse, quoted by Jesus, has haunted me for some time. He says the essence of good comes from God and his nature: "No one is good—except God alone" (Mark 10:18). When we do good, we express God.

As Christ-ians, or little Christs, loving God with all our heart, soul, and mind means we want to do what brings us closer to Jesus and avoid what hinders our intimacy. Doing good does that. Actually, growing closer to Jesus brings a pretty good long-term reward, even if not always a short-term one. Jesus also promised if the world hated and opposed him, they would treat us the same way.

We choose good because we build a reputation for integrity, which can benefit us and our credibility. People are more apt to trust us in spiritual matters.

And we choose good because it has the ultimate reward— we grow in godliness, which is good. "Godliness with contentment is great gain" (1 Timothy 6:6). Committing to good actions brings a great payback. We become content with all the trouble in life. We may not embrace trouble, but we can accept it because our good works have so much more value than the troubles we encounter. It brings the best ROI, or Return on Investment, we can hope for on this planet.

But we must answer this question as individuals: Does acting godly content us? Or do we need human acknowledgment or personal benefit? If the latter, what do we focus on? Ourselves. If the former, the focus goes to God.

As followers of Jesus, let's do the right thing. The good thing. Let's be content expressing God's character, with little thought of short-term consequences, good or bad. Shouldn't godliness be our greatest goal?

KICK-STARTING THE APPLICATION

Think about how you choose to respond to a situation. If you're at all like me, you might evaluate it first to consider the impact it will have on you. Often, what benefits us is worth doing, while what does not bring us a short-term advantage means we're not likely to do it. What does evaluating situations in this way reveal about our hearts? Do we first care about ourselves or about expressing God's character? Are you content with your answers? What practical steps can you take to choose godliness first?

5—CHALLENGE YOURSELF

The apostle Paul told us we need to change, to leave immaturity behind, to challenge our limits, to "become mature, attaining to the whole measure of the *fullness* of Christ. Then we will *no longer be infants* ... Instead ... we will *grow to become in every respect* the mature body of him who is the head, that is, Christ" (Ephesians 4:13–15). Change. Growth. These normal parts of following Jesus will never happen when we're content with mediocrity, when we cling to our current state. Therefore, we must push our limits. Move beyond our comfort zones. Find a new and better normal.

This chapter title refers to a time I moved beyond my comfort zone, by doing an Iron Butt ride—1,000 miles in 24 hours on two wheels at the age of 70. I share the details of this tale in another chapter but will give the motivation for this ride here. If you're not a biker and think of a ride like that as idiocy, I won't argue. A lot of seasoned bikers look at it the same way. But the Iron Butt ride creates a metaphor for all who follow Jesus or are at least intrigued with him.

Long ago, I amplified a popular quote frequently attributed to Frank Sonnenberg: "Step outside your comfort zone. If you don't push your limits, you'll never get better." My version goes, "If we don't push our limits, we'll never learn the true extent of our abilities and motivations and faith." If we don't move beyond our current spiritual status, we remain spiritually immature. To an extent, we unconsciously claim we're so close to perfect we can't get any better. Blasphemy? Perhaps on some level.

At 70, I wanted to discover if I was still tough enough to endure this ride. If I had the courage. But think of the ride as a metaphor about other issues we need to challenge ourselves in. Prayer. Forgiveness. Love. A new ministry. Speaking about Jesus. Studying the Bible more. We may also find areas we need to avoid, like lust or laziness. You can add your own. Since none of us do all these or similar issues as well as we should, we need to extend our limits to grow in these more fully.

In my early years, fear often drove me. I played it safe because failing said something about me—something I didn't want to face. The change would take effort, and like many, I have a lazy streak. Change doesn't always work out for the good, not in a fallen world with fallen people who have an impact on us. Ironically, my obsession with fear only caused it to grow.

Motorcycles contributed significantly to me making these changes. A pushy neighbor forced me to try a short ride, and I liked it. Then the movie *Easy Rider* entranced me with the freedom of the open road, and I bought a bike.

That bike helped start the process of challenging the fears that chained me. Some limits I've been forced to address and move beyond: a deeply imbedded self-will, an independence that has hindered healthy relationships, not dealing with sexual temptation soon and strongly enough, laziness, a fear of public speaking that led into ministry (the next chapter tells that story). Getting several master's degrees that transitioned me out of local ministry after several decades as God led me into broader opportunities. Yeah, the list could go on.

Once I challenged myself, I found a freedom, an exhilaration at discovering my potential. A freedom beyond mediocrity. No more doing the same old, same old. A chance at growing into the person God designed me to become. I received opportunities to impact others more effectively. Challenging myself has led to a life beyond my dreams.

But I added a caveat to my new life theme of challenging oneself: "But if you push yourself unwisely, you die." Let's be real. We often hear today if you dream big enough and work hard enough, you can reach your dreams. That's bull. I'll never be an All-Pro wide receiver in the NFL, not having the speed, size, or the hand-eye coordination. If we push some limits too much, we will fail, and discouragement and depression will overwhelm us. Or we could even die.

So, choose a challenge in the realm of possibility, not of stupidity. On the Iron Butt ride, I pushed my limits strategically. I figured about how many hours it would take, and I'd done those on a shorter ride just two years before. I chose a route on I-15 from Temecula, California, to Dillon, Montana, the first town over 1,000 miles distant. The route was a straight road, very little traffic most of the way, a typical speed limit of 80, with most vehicles moving above that. And I promised my wife I wouldn't sacrifice my life trying to do it. To increase the challenge, I made a room reservation in Dillon but could have stopped easily in Idaho Falls, 140 miles shorter. I left myself an out.

Yeah, I made it—1,080 miles in 16.3 hours. I was exhausted. But when I pulled the Honda into the Motel 6 lot, I smiled. Will I try another? I'm not likely to at 76, especially as some health issues arrived at 75. But honestly, I still have bigger challenges, new or continuing spiritual arenas to address, significant books to write.

But the Iron Butt challenge gave me a small glimpse of what God has in store for those who trust God and challenge themselves:

> No eye has seen, no ear has heard,
>   and no mind has imagined
> what God has prepared
>   for those who love him.
> (1 Corinthians 2:9 NLT)

Remember, the most difficult and meaningful challenges aren't physical, but spiritual. After ten seconds in heaven, having done an Iron Butt at 70 will mean nothing. Are you ready to glimpse how much godlier you can become? I encourage you, accept God's challenge to push your spiritual limits.

KICK-STARTING THE APPLICATION

Think of a time you pushed a limit, and it opened a new realm of life. Why did you push? What role did God play? Do you sense an area or areas God would like you to grow beyond your current limits? If you accept or reject his challenge, what will that say about you? How can you do it strategically? What role will he play in pushing your limits and growing?

6—FIND YOUR LIMITS

In the previous chapter, we examined our need to challenge ourselves, using the slogan "If you don't push your limits, you'll never learn the true extent of your abilities and motivations and faith." I find truth in that slogan and encourage all to wisely and strategically push the possible in their lives. Only when we push our limits can we learn where they are. Otherwise, we can only guess or act in fear or foolishness. Now that we briefly explored limits, let's go deeper and find a caveat.

On my Iron Butt ride back in 2018 at the ripe age of 70, I decided to push myself to discover my endurance limits on a motorcycle. I planned a projected ride of 1,080 miles in 24 hours. I started strong, leaving my Temecula home in the dark at 4 a.m., with a brief stop in Barstow for gas, coffee, and breakfast at Mickie D's, a quick gas stop in Vegas, then arrived in Cedar City, Utah, 465 miles later, in six and one half hours. That mileage was almost half the total, but I felt pretty tired. So, I took an early and longer-than-planned lunch break at a converted train station: a nice craft beer to relax, a strong coffee to counteract the beer, and a tasty Cubano sandwich. My next target was Provo, 210 miles down the road ... about three hours away.

But at 170 miles, the tiredness returned, so 22 miles short of Provo, I grabbed a snack, gas, and rest in Santaquin. My pace was slowing down a little. I discovered my early and hard start impacted my ability to handle the longer segments I'd planned. And I was 70. So I adjusted, and the next three segments ended at 132 miles, 155, and 140, mostly based on gas locations. Optimal segments for me were those under 150 miles. For the first half, I averaged 72 mph, including stops. But for the last half, 615 miles, I averaged 62 mph. Yes, I made it to Dillon, Montana, 1,080 miles in a total time of 16.3 hours, traveling an average of 66 mph. The key term: I made it. I succeeded because I recognized some very real limits and tweaked my plans, realizing those longer segments exceeded my abilities to finish them.

The same principle applies to following Jesus. Yes, we push our limits, finding both the extent of our abilities and motivations and faith. Keep in mind, a LOT of these lessons must be learned the hard way, by making mistakes and feeling pain. But we find some true limits. And we listen to them. Here are some of mine—you might share them, or you might have ones of your own.

Temptations impact us all. We have two primary tools to deal with them: strength or escape. First Corinthians 10:13 tells us, "No temptation has overtaken you except what is common to mankind. And God is faithful; he will not let you be tempted *beyond what you can bear*. But when you are tempted, he will also *provide a way out* so that you can endure it." Only when we know our strength limits can we know when to run.

Getting into soft porn some years back changed how I deal with temptation, and running often provides an escape from that temptation for me. Failing in a temptation can make us stronger—or weaker—in that area. We need to factor in that change.

Abilities and gifts are given to all, but none of us are talented in all arenas. Sometimes, our youthful enthusiasm and energy allow us to function in areas we're not suited for, but spending too much time in those areas drains us. We should instead focus on what God designed us to do.

But sometimes those talents change or are hidden. I did so poorly giving oral reports in school, my mom and my academic counselor made me take a speech course. On the first day of the course, the teacher said we could get out of the class if we joined the debate team. I did, thinking we'd sit around a table and argue. He never mentioned debate tournaments would require me to speak 100 times as much as the class would have. Then Pepperdine offered me a debate scholarship, so the onerous journey in speaking continued.

A bad call? Yes, based on my limited ability to speak and my fear of it. But I learned my limits exceeded my earlier evaluation of them—the bulk of my working life has been in oral communication, as a pastor and educator and speaker. Go figure! God has quite a sense of humor as he guides our lives.

Energy levels vary due to many factors: age, levels of exertion, emotional issues, even an adrenaline dump after a great event. We need to listen to our body and soul. God commanded a day of rest. He knows our energy is limited. If I hadn't extended my Iron Butt stops, I wouldn't have made it.

Knowledge limits us, since none of us are omniscient like God. I sometimes watch *Shark Tank*, where I've heard the line, "You don't know what you don't know." We need a God-given humility to realize we don't know as much as we thought we did when we were teenagers. We assume things and often pay the price for not learning more. Now in my 70s, I feel I know less all the time—I've discovered how much information is out there. Before we plan to stretch ourselves, we need the knowledge to make the best plan.

Faith itself is limited due to our human nature, failings, and weaknesses. I appreciate the passage from Romans 13:11 (NLT): "Wake up, for our salvation is nearer now than when we first believed." Yes, salvation comes when we accept Jesus as Savior and Lord through faith, yet it comes in its fullness on Jesus's return. Our faith grows in strength as we nurture it, challenge it, and grow closer to our Savior, but never is it omnipotent.

Yes, those are just a few of our limits. Learn to recognize yours, listen, and adapt. Finish the ride.

KICK-STARTING THE APPLICATION

Do you have the limits above? What others? How have you found and followed your limits? Did the pain of the lesson show its importance? Where does God fit into the process? Can you think of a limit you need to stretch?

7—UNEXPECTED PROVISION

By Jim Davis, retired schoolteacher, musician, outdoorsman

Back in 1974, a long-distance solo motorcycle ride on a 1973 Honda CL350 could have gone horribly wrong—and did. My motor purred on the asphalt from Southern California to northern New Mexico as I traveled to join nine others serving on a mission trip.

For two and a half weeks, we worked at a community recreation center in Peñasco, New Mexico. We did arts and crafts, played board and card games, and ran outside activities with the children and teens each day. This interaction brought great fun and new friendships among the children and adults.

But having to leave sooner than the others, I packed my gear on the bike and headed home on Saturday, to be back at work Monday.

While riding through Santa Fe and coasting to a stop at a light, the bike began to shake, sputter, stumble, and lose power. When we came to a stop, the engine completely shut off. The starter button wouldn't turn it over. The kick-starter wouldn't even budge. My heart sank as the bike was only six months old. What was going on? I moved the bike to the shoulder and pondered what to do. I needed a Honda dealer. The Yellow Pages revealed one about a half mile away.

I pushed it there and explained what happened. The mechanics checked the oil dipstick, which came up completely dry. The engine had seized from lack of oil. How? The bike only had 3,000 miles and was serviced before I left. How could it possibly have gone through three quarts of oil that soon? I was stuck. I couldn't wait for Honda to decide to fix it, nor did I have money to pay for the repair. So, they agreed to my request to keep the bike with them until I could arrange transportation.

Hitchhiking back to Peñasco, 70 miles away, seemed the only option ... something I had never done before. A little scared? Yes.

To my great surprise, three very different people picked me up. An older man gave me a ride to Española, about 25 miles north. Then a husband and wife and their daughter let me ride in the back of their pickup for another 30 miles. But Peñasco lay 15 miles farther, which led to a small miracle. A young man picked me up and dropped me off one mile from the house I just left that morning. The crew's astonished looks greeted me when I walked back into the house.

But how would I get home? My parents weren't available to help. Fortunately, another crew member with her father and boyfriend were leaving to go home the next day. Their Ford Ranchero had a truck bed in the back where my bike and I "rode" home together, side by side, just missing one day of work.

God protected and provided for me throughout this disaster. He protected me from injury with a slow-speed engine failure and provided safe people who picked me up along the route back. He also provided a repair shop nearby, rides back to Peñasco, and transportation for my bike and me back home. He is God, my Provider.

Jim's story addresses one of the thorniest issues people have with God. Pain. Suffering. Hard times. How can a loving and powerful God not take it all away? Rabbi Harold Kushner, in his 1981 book *When Bad Things Happen to Good People*, suggested an all-powerful God *could* eliminate pain and suffering, and a loving God *would*. Therefore, God is either not loving or not all-powerful. You can't have both. To preserve a God of love, Kushner diminished the power of God: a loving God would end it, but he can't.

The prof in my university logic class, Dr. Arlie J. Hoover, would have labeled Kushner's conclusion the Horns of a Dilemma fallacy, where an argument has two contrasting points and only one can be chosen, like being told at a buffet of 100 items you can only choose zucchini or soup. Either God is loving or powerful, but not both. You treat this fallacy by either breaking one of the horns (proving it wrong) or by finding another option in between them. Really, an easy logical fallacy to refute.

We call that process being free moral agents. Or we choose, and each choice includes good or bad consequences, for ourselves or others a long way downstream. Because of the choices of Adam and Eve, we live in a fallen world. Romans 8:22 tells us "the whole creation has been groaning as in the pains of childbirth."

God gives us the ability to make genuine decisions with genuine results; otherwise, we'd be Stepford Christians. God wants followers who freely choose him, as Joshua expressed: "*Choose* for yourselves this day whom you will serve, whether the gods your ancestors served beyond the

Euphrates, or the gods of the Amorites, in whose land you are living. But as for me and my household, *we will serve the Lord*" (Joshua 24:15).

Kushner's quandary of just two choices about God gets resolved with realizing God chooses to limit the expression of his power to allow us valid free choice.

But even so, this loving God intervenes: "For God so loved the world that he gave his one and only Son, that whoever believes in him shall not perish but have eternal life" (John 3:16). He encourages us with his presence in the darkest times:

> Even though I walk
>   through the darkest valley,
> I will fear no evil,
>   for you are with me;
> your rod and your staff,
>   they comfort me.
> (Psalm 23:4)

Along with that comfort, God also works to redeem the worst of times: "And we know that in *all things God works for the good* of those who love him, who have been called according to his purpose" (Romans 8:28). We may not always know how or why, though. Job never learned why he suffered so much, but he trusted in God's love.

And the life he gives his followers far surpasses the worst a fallen world can throw at us.

Kick-Starting the Application

Have you been frustrated when God doesn't take away the hard times and sufferings? Do you sense his presence and comfort during them? Do you see how choice works in bringing pain and hard times?

MORE GOD, MOTORCYCLES, AND OPEN ROAD

Jim Davis was born in SoCal and began riding at 19, starting on a Honda CB175, eventually moving up to a Yamaha 750. He no longer rides but loves traveling out on the open road. He now lives in Murrieta, California, and helps lead worship at a nearby church.

8—DODGING OBSTACLES

I hesitate to call it the "Alaska Trip" because it revealed so many previously unseen facets of the jeweled orb we call earth. Rich and I connected above Seattle, Washington, headed north to Prince George in British Columbia, then west to Stewart, British Columbia, and Hyder, Alaska. The last 40 miles astounded us with glaciers and rivers streaming from cliffs. Oh yes—and grizzlies to spot and avoid.

Alaska's beauty wasn't the only drawing card—I needed an Alaska trip for my quest to ride in all 50 states. Alaska was number 47, leaving just three for me at the time.

After we left Alaska, we headed south where Rich and I picked up Jerry around Seattle. Rich then headed east to his home in South Dakota, and Jerry and I turned south to meet Mick and Brad and explore Mt. Rainer. Utterly stupendous.

Once more we headed south, until Jerry spun off north to his home in Salem, Oregon. Mick, Brad, and I visited the most majestic cathedral I've experienced, located on Highway 1 in Northern California on the Avenue of the Giants. We slowly cruised through redwoods that crept to the very edge of the road and provided a canopy of boughs that kept us cool. And in awe. Then Brad spotted a side road we'd never taken, Mattole Road to the Big Tree Grove. We'd never even heard of either Mattole or the Grove, so we yielded to temptation. As I recall, we didn't even pull out a map, although Brad had it on Waze.

If Highway 1 was narrow, Mattole was just a faint curving line that dodged between redwoods rather than bulldozing them. A couple of times a car approached the opposite way, and the space got quite tight. I felt like a very slow slalom skier on the bike, swerving around redwoods and potholes. That slowness proved wise when a doe jumped out five feet in front of me. She bounded 20 feet up the slope, then stopped to look at this strange creature perched on a yellow Goldwing with an American flag on the helmet. Another doe waited for her, and as I grabbed my cell camera, Brad said a third crossed the road ahead of me.

That marvelous road had a lot of obstacles to avoid: moving deer, stationary redwoods, and approaching cars. And it taught me something about following Jesus. We face obstacles. Others' expectations of us—that don't match either our nature or Scripture. Our weak areas—laziness, lust, self-centeredness, out-of-control ambition, or others. Complacency—one that allows us to settle for less than God's best. All these obstacles can bring damage and cause us to fall short.

So, we dodge them. Granted, we can't always. A few years ago, a doe jumped in front of Brad near these mountains. He couldn't avoid T-boning her, an accident which required a life flight to the nearest trauma hospital to save his life. The deer didn't make it. But we do what we can. First Peter 5:8 says, "Be alert and of sober mind. Your enemy the devil prowls around like a roaring lion looking for someone to devour." We develop the habit of continual awareness so we can identify obstacles to dodge. And like on Mattole Road, we don't just look five feet in front of us—we look farther down the road for the consequences of each decision.

We want to arrive alive and healthy, with a smile.

MORE GOD, MOTORCYCLES, AND OPEN ROAD | 33
Kick-Starting the Application

What are some of the obstacles you face? What strategies work? Which don't? Would it help you to intentionally craft some plans to see and respond to them? Maybe take some time to specifically identify some obstacles and create a game plan for them. Would it help you to get an accountability partner?

9—TO CRUISE OR NOT TO CRUISE

For my first 100,000 miles on a bike, I rode old style: twist and adjust the throttle to match the need for speed. Frankly, that method caused some cramping on long rides, yet back in those days we had few options. Then my third bike, a '78 Goldwing, had a throttle lock I loved, a spring clamp that held the throttle at the speed you liked. You would get to the speed you wanted and lock the throttle with your right thumb. The clamp held it there, saving your hand and wrist muscles.

But it didn't control the speed, just the position, so when you arrived at a hill, you slowed down going up and sped up going down. You'd have to turn the lock off, accelerate, or slow down to the desired throttle position, then reset it. Again. Better, but not ideal.

Then I saw a Cramp Buster, a lever that attaches to the outside end of the throttle. You rest the butt of your hand on the lever instead of gripping it with your whole hand. This position makes going around town much easier. The Cramp Buster has helped to ease the grip and used with the throttle lock made long rides more comfortable.

But I still envied my Goldwing friends with REAL cruise control. They could find and set their speed, and the cruise control held it, regardless of the climb. Now I loved my

ST1300 more than their Wings. My bike maneuvered better, was faster, got better mileage, and looked cooler. But it just had the throttle lock and Cramp Buster, and we took some very long rides.

When my balance declined with age, my ST tempted me to take a corner I could no longer do safely. Knowing the time had arrived for a change, I picked up a used Wing. With cruise.

On my first long ride with the Wing, a 3,700 mile ride to Alaska, much of it on interstates to eat the miles, I loved it. Especially the plus and minus buttons to adjust the speed. The ease of long rides amazed and captivated me. So much so that when the Wing got totaled after three years, I got the son of the ST1300, a Honda CTX1300, and had an aftermarket cruise control installed. It works great, and I'm one happy biker.

On that trip. I followed the advice of a previous rider on the 40-mile leg from Kitwanga Junction, British Columbia, to Stewart, British Columbia, right next to Hyder, Alaska: set it at 50, enjoy the scenery, and watch for grizzlies. The cruise allowed me to do that, and I loved the experience.

I learned many miles back to always pay attention while riding, but the cruise taught me a new lesson. It's great to use on straight roads or long, sweeping curves. It gives better gas mileage, saves my wrist, and is easier for those behind to follow my now consistent speed. And I don't need to pay quite as much attention.

But. Yeah, there's just about always a "but." I swear when a tight turn came up, one where I couldn't see the entire curve, that sucker sped up the bike. I'd have to quickly brake or pull in the clutch to release the control. The situations got a bit dicey a few times, so I learned in the winding mountains to anticipate that. Most times, I just turned it off. And using the cruise control was just flat-out

MORE GOD, MOTORCYCLES, AND OPEN ROAD | 37

dangerous in cities, so the cruise control I loved, I couldn't always use.

The hook here? Think of the spiritual life like riding with the cruise control as a metaphor since it does give some helpful tips.

Tip 1: Craft a plan on where you want to end up. Some of you may share my failure to put enough intentionality into my faith in Jesus. Oh, we want to get to heaven, to be godly, but we kind of wing it. On a bike, winging it is a good way to run out of gas. Part of my plan to maximize riding was using the cruise. Paul did the same: "I wanted to visit you on my way to Macedonia and to come back to you from Macedonia, and then to have you send me on my way to Judea. Was I fickle when I intended to do this?" (2 Corinthians 1:16–17). He put thought and prayer into his plans, but he also followed the next tip.

Tip 2: Adapt to changing situations. Paul modeled turning off the cruise on some roads: "Now when I went to Troas to preach the gospel of Christ and found that the Lord had opened a door for me, I still had no peace of mind, because I did not find my brother Titus there. So I *said goodbye to them and went on to Macedonia*" (2 Corinthians 2:12–13). Paul had a fine plan, and God supported it by opening a door. But Titus didn't show up, so Paul went in the opposite way. In riding and in life, we pay close attention to what's happening, and we change plans when we need to. Then we lean on the next tip.

Tip 3: Trust in God's presence in the new plan. I still turn on the cruise as needed, and it works. Paul experienced the same on his new plan, as we see in the next verse: "But thanks be to God, who *always leads us ... in Christ's triumphal procession*" (2 Corinthians 2:14). Even though he turned away from the door God opened, he realized God always leads. I suspect he was familiar with one of my life verses, Proverbs 16:9: "We can make our plans, but the LORD determines our steps" (NLT).

Nice to know no matter the wrong turns, bad turns, or changing plans—nothing fazes him.

KICK-STARTING THE APPLICATION

How intentional are you in planning your spiritual life? How loosely do you hold those plans? Are there some areas where you just cruise and don't pay full attention? Has that inattention ever bitten you on your butt? How do you identify times to change your plans or accept God changing them?

10—SEE THE BIG PICTURE

If you do an internet search for a pic of the Motel 6 in Dillon, Montana, you're not apt to rush to hotels.com to make a reservation. The sparse but spacious room was affordable with a good bed and an acceptable shower—my main requirements for that night, along with coffee for the morning. The surrounding country looked amazing. But this "just a room for the night" represented a major goal.

Even though my great-great uncle, Luke Short, and my grandfather, Percy Rice, both probably passed through Dillon, the town itself wasn't my goal. The day began with a self-generated challenge to push my limits and survive an Iron Butt ride, over 1,000 miles in 24 hours on a motorcycle. My goal was 1,080 miles, not Dillon. Dillon just happened to be the first town after passing 1,000 miles.

But a lesson I gave as a college prof played a key role in understanding, planning, and executing the ride: the difference between terminal and instrumental goals. Let's explore that concept and then apply it to the ride on the bike and our walk with Jesus. Terminal goals are an end in themselves—they don't lead to other goals. Eating chocolate every day is a terminal goal of mine. It's not a means to another goal—I just enjoy it. Instrumental goals help us reach a higher goal. For me, walking and working out most days are instrumental—they lead to better health and function, but I don't particularly delight in them.

My Iron Butt ride incorporated both terminal and instrumental goals. One thousand miles was an instrument to challenge myself and find my limits—the terminal goal for the trip.

We often consider terminal goals as what we want to achieve in our lifetime, and they vary in importance. My highest terminal goal—one that tops all others—is that when I die, I want to meet Jesus, see a smile on his face, and hear "Ya done good, kid!" (see Matthew 25:21). Loving God and people is instrumental in reaching that terminal goal. I had no desire on the ride to take a needless risk and die prematurely, which would result in me not touching as many people as possible and not being able to take care of my wife.

Part of my instrumental process involved questioning if it was possible to do the 1,000 miles and arrive alive. Luke 14:28–30, a passage about goals, applies here: "Suppose one of you wants to build a tower. Won't you first sit down and estimate the cost to see if you have enough money to complete it? For if you lay the foundation and are not able to finish it, everyone who sees it will ridicule you, saying, 'This person began to build and wasn't able to finish.'"

The goal of building a tower stands as a metaphor for just about any of our goals, mostly terminal but also instrumental. Don't be stupid. Strategize how to accomplish them. So, in my case, I had to ask myself if an Iron Butt was possible.

I thought so. I had ridden the required number of hours in one day just the year before. I had a bike ideally suited for 1,080 miles in one day. I planned out the route in detail with gas and food stops, leaving margin for the unexpected. Yes, the unexpected occurred, multiple times. And yes, I had promised my wife I wouldn't push so hard it risked my life and health. How stupid to cover 980 miles, fall short of 1,000, and die from falling asleep or driving too fast. I kept the big picture in mind: survival. I wanted to sleep in the Motel 6 room, not on a coroner's slab.

So, arriving safely trumped not arriving. Period. I may be a bit crazy, but I try to avoid stupid. I didn't want to see Jesus and hear, "Tim, that was a foolish risk, and you lost. You could have done much more on earth."

Now, let's get personal. Maybe we all should think ahead: What are our terminal spiritual goals? What instrumental goals can help us reach them? Frankly, this type of planning wasn't that important earlier in my life. I kind of flew by the seat of my pants, and I regret that. God has led my life; I've served him, but I might have been more effective with more intentionality.

Before we craft goals, I suggest we prepare by spending time in prayer and looking through Jesus's words in John 14:1 to 17:26 to align our spirit with his. After 50 years of following him, here is my primary terminal life goal: to know God and to love him with all my being. My second primary terminal goal is to actively love people as I love myself and to strive to benefit them. You can find some passages that support those goals in John 17:3 and Matthew 22:26–40.

For whatever terminal goals you have, and just about all instrumentals, maybe hold onto them with a loose grip. By that, I mean leave room for God to guide, lead, and disrupt. He is God, after all. I do love the NLT's version of Proverbs 16:9: "We can make our plans, but the Lord determines our steps."

I've found his determining has saved me from a boatload of grief. Many times.

For those who don't follow Jesus, I encourage you to work this process of goals as well. And maybe one instrumental goal of yours could be to explore God to see if he's worth giving your life to.

KICK-STARTING THE APPLICATION

Have you chosen a terminal goal for your life? If not, do you have a sense of purpose or just existence? What do you think God would want for you? If you do have one, do you regularly evaluate your instrumental goals for how effectively they help reach your terminal? What changes in both terminal and instrumental might be helpful?

11—SEASONS

After more than 20 years of riding motorcycles, multiple trips with two brothers-in-law, and then becoming a founding member of the Gray Hogs, Mick finally decided his season of riding had reached its end after our 2014 ride to Taos, New Mexico. Then 74, he had ridden the entire Western United States and much of the Midwest. Two buffalo strolled by both sides of his bike in Yellowstone, each within three feet of him. He bagged his bucket list city of Banff in Canada and basked in the pools at Radium Hot Springs just below. In all those years and miles, he'd never had an accident, so he thought wisdom suggested he quit while he was still ahead and healthy. The odds of not going down were changing, with no reason to keep pushing his luck.

To show his commitment and to reduce temptation, he gave his Honda Goldwing to his son-in-law up in Northern California. His riding days ended. He looked back on many miles, a lot of trips with no problems, and a slew of great stories and memories.

But his wife noticed how excited he got when bikes came up in conversations, how the stories got retold with a smile. Her take? "This man is not ready to give it up." Our group rode up to Oregon the next summer, but Mick didn't miss it—he drove his car up to Northern California and borrowed his bike back from his son-in-law. A smile stretched his face as we rode through backcountry Oregon roads and then up to Mt. St. Helens in Washington. The Mick was back, doing what he loved.

His son-in-law wanted to join next year's ride, so Mick picked up a Honda Shadow 1100. A fine street bike but too low geared for long rides, and the bike crawled going uphill on mountain roads. He rode the Shadow another year, then came back to his favored ride, a Goldwing. In 2019 he completed a two-week, 3,700-mile ride, ending a week before his 80th birthday. Even at 80, the season hadn't changed.

In part due to COVID, in part to his endurance, the 2020 and 2021 trips were shorter, one up the California coast and mountains, and the other tracing the Sierra passes from one side to the other. On the last night, at the dinner table with Jerry, Brad, and me, he announced his riding days were over. A seven-year season since he first gave it up. So, what can we all learn from Mick?

Life comes in many seasons, not just the four we think of. My mom's philosophy about change came from a popular phrase in the King James Bible, "It came to pass." This phrase is used a grand total of 457 times! Mom added a little to her version: "It came to pass; it didn't come to stay." Yes, she knew her take didn't represent the meaning of the text, but it captured truth about life. Not all good things are permanent—some come to pass. Robert Frost captured that in his poem with a title that matches the last line: "So dawn goes down to day. / Nothing gold can stay."

I viewed my two years in Taos as gold, living in a log cabin for a year in the mountains and then in town for another, but God brought me to Taos to nudge me back into ministry—a grace gift intended to pass into something for his kingdom. A season, not forever.

Change is one of the constants in life. God called Paul and Barnabas to be a phenomenally effective mission team, until they had a disagreement and parted. That season ended. On Palm Sunday, the crowd acclaimed Jesus as a Savior from God, but by the end of the week, a crowd (very possibly a different group) clamored for his crucifixion. The season of acclaim ended in five days.

Our role is to carefully sense the seasons of change and navigate them with grace and faith. At one church, I should have resigned sooner—I'd led them through a lot of changes and should have left it earlier for a fresh guy to enjoy the newness. Another time, I should have stayed longer and helped resolve some issues that had long plagued the church. My two years in Taos delighted me, but God designed them as a season to move me into the next.

So, some tips. Embrace change as a constant and enjoy the opportunity to grow, gain new experiences, and get stretched. Work through seasons by bathing them in grace and wise input from others. My worst mistakes in changes came from not taking time to consult with wise friends.

And leave room for God to work. This verse influenced me decades back, and I'm still learning to use it: "We can make our plans, but the Lord determines our steps" (Proverbs 16:9 NLT).

Make plans, but let God change them. Looking back over the decades, I better see his hand guiding and protecting me from my own plans and desires. Only later can I see how he had to move one aspect I enjoyed to bring something better.

Also, let's get our ego out of the way a bit. The brother of Jesus cautioned us in James 4:15–16 about how we should make our plans: "'If it is the Lord's will, we will live and do this or that.' As it is, you boast in your arrogant schemes. All such boasting is evil" (see also verses 13–14). We usually know less than we think we do.

Back in 2015, Mick listened to his wife and his heart and gained seven years of riding before that season ended for the last time.

Kick-Starting the Application

Looking back, how well have you navigated changes? What helped you navigate them? What caused you some grief? Do you sense any changes God or life might be hinting are on their way? How can you better prepare for them? If they arrive, how can you better work with them? How involved is God in your decisions and reactions? How can you involve him more?

12—SERENITY OR STRESS

We all face sources of stress. Jobs. Relationships. Family. Finances. Neighbors. Life isn't always a stroll in the park, but perhaps we can extract some tips from a bike trip that carried several sources of stress and learn how we can choose serenity instead.

In 2013, our biker group rode from SoCal and Oregon to Idaho and then Montana, with Glacier National Park as our objective. Jerry and Mick had ridden there about 10 years before, and while they both raved about a return, Jerry expressed some unease about the sheer drop-off into a canyon next to the road.

In Missoula, we toured the Presbyterian church Norman Maclean's father pastored in the book and movie *A River Runs Through It*. I asked if I could stand in the pulpit, and standing there deeply touched my soul with its sacred history.

The next day, we headed north to Kalispell along Highway 93. Our map showed green dots for great scenery along the road. But 20 miles before Seeley Lake, site of the Maclean's getaway cabin, we ran into heavy rain. I had the lead then. My ST1300 had a narrow windshield compared to the ones on the Goldwings the rest of the crew sported, and the lack of visibility had me squinting my eyes and clenching my hands on the bars. The ride was not a fun despite the beauty when the skies cleared.

We arrived on the season-opening day for the Going-to-the-Sun Road, so we left Kalispell early, about 7 a.m., to avoid the crowd. As I recall, the 30 miles featured a temp not much higher, and my body tightened in the chill.

We slowly cruised east along what they called McDonald Creek, but it met the standards of a California river. My blog, *Unconventional*, features a pic of me on a bridge, and I wished I'd brought a trout rod along. A large mountain ridge rose up on our right, but the easy cruise ended at the Loop. This road, barely etched into the mountainside, did a 170-degree reverse and began climbing and switch backing. Jerry knew his road. It was narrow, and if you went over, you'd likely fall a thousand feet before touching anything. Riding the loop was a bit intimidating, and I shuddered more than once.

Part of the stress came from gauging our altitude gain by watching that huge mountain to our right, enjoying the majestic scenery, and trying to keep an eye on the road at least some of the time. I think some call it multitasking. We took a break at Logan Pass and grabbed some coffee to warm our insides, then retraced our route. We had laughed on the way up at the Weeping Wall, where the entire cut seeped water from the snow melt, with three streams flowing down the rock. The middle one reached the center of the road, and we chuckled as we saw people in an open convertible coming down trying to dodge the water.

At the time, I never thought of our need to do the same on the way back. Graciously, several cars saw our plight and stopped so we could slide over into their lane to escape the onslaught of very cold water. Well, most of it anyway—we still felt some spray.

Those two days provided a lot of stressors—a downpour that kept us from seeing the road, the bitter cold in the morning, the sheer cliff the road rose above, and the need to pay attention. But here's the kicker. Through it all, I felt serenity. Some of my muscles tightened, but I didn't experience any mental or emotional stress. Why? Some bikers call it "wind therapy."

One team of researchers found that to gain the maximum mental, emotional, and spiritual benefits from being outside, we need to spend at least 120 minutes a week outdoors.[1] Another study, done by UCLA, focused specifically on how riding enables us to replace stress with serenity. The researchers discovered riders' stress levels decreased by 28 percent during a 20-minute motorcycle ride. Their heartbeats increased by 11 percent, their adrenaline by 27 percent, and their alertness grew.[2]

But how does wind therapy work? Theories vary, but bikers merely say wind washes away worries and stress. I can buy that explanation but let me add one more factor: humility. Riding through massive mountains and forests amid glaciers and lakes and rivers reveals the majesty of a Creator—one who appreciates beauty, whose power and love transcend anything I've experienced. The distance in type and power between God and me causes the humility.

Realize this decreased stress doesn't eliminate the issues, but being outdoors, especially for an extended period, lets me know I'm not alone. I'm immersed in the works of a magnificent Deity, who created this world for people and gave us the use of it. Knowing he loves and cares makes me feel like the smallest kid on the block—with a BIG, big brother. If God can create such a marvelous, beautiful, and practical world, then he can get me through life.

I know many of you don't ride, have no interest in it, and never will. Honestly, that's fine. But think about the concept of wind therapy, the benefits of being outdoors, maybe just with a walk in a neighborhood park. Even more significantly, how do you find your serenity, that double shot of God's love and majesty? We'll each find that differently, but let's get out in God's world and see him better than we do in man-made city scenes.

God not only gave us the world, but he gave us a choice: Serenity or stress? We all face stress, but getting outdoors, enjoying his creation, can bring serenity to us all. Our choice.

Kick-Starting the Application

Do you notice the causes of stress in your life? Do you see the glory and majesty and love of God expressed in creation? How often do you get outside to enjoy it and gain serenity? How can you expand your time outdoors?

13—RUBY AND ME

By Dan DeWitt, pastor, biker

I was talking with Ruby one night. She said she was getting a little restless. Honda called her a Valkyrie for a reason: she was a dragon at heart. I called her Ruby for a different reason. Sure, she's red and black, but I don't just call her Ruby because she is red. I call her Ruby because she's a lot like my grandmother. Grandma's name was Ruby, and like Grandma, Ruby is a little bit wide, sits low to the ground, and likes to go fast. Grandma's days of terrorizing teenagers on the boulevard have long since come to an end, but my little Ruby rumbles on.

Ruby told me she was tired of seeing Illinois cornfields. She was a dragon and was longing to spread her wings. The air was warm. The days were long. Sure, Hurricane Ida was roaming around in the Gulf of Mexico, but we decided to throw caution to the wind.

Ruby and I put the cornfields in our rearview mirror and set our compass toward motorcycle mecca: the Tail of the Dragon. The Dragon is a road with 318 corners of true bliss compressed into an 11-mile section of twisties on the border of Tennessee and North Carolina. It was just what Ruby needed, and I was delighted she asked me to come along for the ride.

And boy, was it a great ride! Ruby dragged her pegs all the way through the Dragon, making sure no one passed her as she showed her stuff, twisting and turning and loving each precious mile. With every corner she passed, her smile got bigger and bigger. She was having the time of her life. Her Dragon heart was fully alive.

Ruby enjoyed the Tail of the Dragon so much we couldn't stop. We kept going farther and farther into the Appalachians through the Blue Ridge Parkway. She stopped quite often at scenic overlooks, soaking in the vistas of the Smoky Mountains, happy there was not a cornfield in sight. Farther and farther she flew through Kentucky, Tennessee, and North Carolina. Nothing could hold her back.

Nothing, that is, except for Hurricane Ida, which was determined to douse the flame burning bright in Ruby's heart. The mighty Ruby dragon couldn't match Ida's torrential rains. Ruby eventually had to seek shelter as she waited for Ida to move on toward New England. But Ruby couldn't be held back for long. As soon as Ida turned her attention away, Ruby set her sights on Virginia and then on through Ohio and Indiana.

I was talking with Ruby last night. She agreed the time spent soaring through the Appalachians has made it easier to live with the cornfields of Illinois. After I tucked her in, I think I heard her talking in her sleep about the Rocky Mountains. Who knows? Maybe Ruby is dreaming about the next adventure for her and me.

My first time reading Ecclesiastes 3:11 shocked me: "He has also *set eternity* in the human heart." The concept of eternity doesn't seem to fit into our flawed humanity, but it's become a favored verse for its affirmation of mankind's special place to God. Then I studied John 17:3: "Now this is *eternal life*: that they may know you, the only true God, and Jesus Christ, whom you have sent." I discovered eternal life or eternity doesn't just mean living forever, but living with fewer limits, having an expansive life. Eternal life transcends the typical physical life, and it begins the moment we know Jesus as Savior and Lord.

This more encompassing view of eternity seems to explain Jabez's prayer: "Oh, that you would bless me and *enlarge my territory!*" (1 Chronicles 4:10). Enlarging his territory was not a promise from God, but a prayer coming from the heart of a God follower that reveals an expansive desire within the souls of people. Something in our God-given nature causes us to yearn to grow, to develop, to expand, to improve. God gave us the earth to develop it for human life.

I suspect this trait causes us to grab onto the concept of adventure, push our limits, and risk safety for the better. Maybe biking serves as a metaphor for the adventurous life in Christ. Bikes expand the territory we see. They expand our sense of awe about God's creation. They come with added risk, no doubt about that, but they expand our lives.

Riding remains central for me at age 76, having ridden 270,000 miles on my butt and in all 50 states. Yet I've scheduled 2024's big ride and am exploring options for 2025. But eternal life transcends motorcycles. And as much as the pursuit of biking adventure benefits our lives, pursuing God brings a far more significant life.

Like with any adventure, knowing God comes with some costs. Some risks. Disruption of a comfortable life. Sacrificing some good parts of our lives for better ones. Losing friends who don't comprehend the changes in our values and behaviors. Putting our loyalty to him above all others.

And knowing God comes with some difficulties: "And without faith it is impossible to please God, because anyone who comes to him must *believe that he exists* and that he rewards those who *earnestly seek him*" (Hebrews 11:6). Believing he exists is relatively easy, but earnestly seeking him requires effort. Time spent in the searching. Having doubts. Learning how to answer some doubts. Learning some doubts won't likely be solved this side of heaven.

But oh, what a ride we get! Always remember, he does reward those who join in the adventure, who leave behind the okay life for the one Jesus offers: "I came so they can have real and *eternal life, more and better life than they ever dreamed of*" (John 10:10 MSG).

Kick-Starting the Application

On a scale of one to ten, where does your overall desire for adventure fit? On the same scale, where does your willingness for adventure in pursuing God fit? What keeps you from seeking him more earnestly?

Dan DeWitt has been riding motorcycles since he was 12 years old. His current ride is a 2000 Honda Valkyrie. When not riding, he enjoys spending time with family and friends. He also serves as pastor of the First Baptist Church of Rantoul, Illinois (https://fbcrantoul.org). You can find Dan at https://www.facebook.com/FBCRantoul.

14—WHEN BIKING ISN'T ENOUGH

Not long after the release of the previous biker devo, *God, a Motorcycle, and the Open Road,* Moody Radio NW invited me to do an interview, arranged by Don Otis of Veritas Communications. Right after the show, a Montana listener emailed me and recommended a gorgeous stretch of asphalt that skirted Bull Lake. That sounded familiar, so I pulled out my Montana map, and ironically, just the summer before, I'd ridden that road with Jerry. The scenery did impress us, and we stopped several times along the way. Images of Bull Lake invade my mind as I'm writing these words.

I mentioned my Bull Lake ride to Don, and he said he'd recently hiked in that area to Rock Lake, a gorgeous lake only accessible by trail. Worst of all, he sent some pics. Only in our dreams could our touring bikes have taken us there.

But this interaction expanded my thinking. I love bikes and long tours—their freedom on the open road, the unobstructed vistas, being directly in God's creation and not sheltered in steel. Smelling new-mown hay, the tang of pine forests, and more. But bikes can't take me everywhere I'd like to go. Like this Rock Lake. Like to the backcountry trout streams I love. As much as the roads give us access to a lot of country, they limit us as well, like railroad tracks limit trains.

So, perhaps those of us who explore need to broaden our tools.

Walking—and I've worn out more than one pair of hiking boots—balances slow speed with the greatest ability to see details. Hiking has given me access to great places and experiences that otherwise I would not have had.

Bicycles go faster than feet alone. Riding them, we still see a lot but are typically limited to trails and roads. I still remember racing my bicycle down the steep Airplane Hill on Signal Hill in Long Beach, reaching a scary but exhilarating 45 mph.

Motorcycles cover yet more ground at a higher speed, require less physical exertion, and immerse the rider in nature. However, they innately carry more danger. Cars offer more protection and can carry much more gear but offer less visibility. Trains cover longer distances and give some great scenery but have limited routes. Even so, some trains, like the Durango to Silverton route take us to places only accessed by rafting the Animas River or hiking a lot.

Planes let us cover distances much faster than earlier travelers could have dreamed of and give a God's-eye view but provide little detail. Plus, for the last 20 years, the required early arrival for plane travel has added to the total travel time.

I guess I'm saying as much as I love motorcycles and long tours, I want to avoid being a one-dimensional traveler. The other options also carry value.

Maybe we also need to avoid being one-dimensional followers who focus on one primary arena of faith. We sometimes do that—almost obsessing on relationships or Bible knowledge or evangelism or serving or leading. We focus on one and ignore other essential dimensions of faith. We can too easily lose balance, like a weightlifter who only works on his forearms and looks like Popeye the Sailor Man. Maybe we should take a variety of routes to work out our whole spiritual body.

But we need to distinguish among different dimensions of faith and different methods we serve in our faith. We have varying spiritual gifts, experiences, and talents, and God will use us uniquely in how we serve him, according to Romans 12:6–8: "*We have different gifts*, according to the grace given us. If a man's gift is prophesying, let him *use it*." Paul continues in these three verses with the gifts of serving, teaching, encouraging, contributing to the needs of others, leadership, and showing mercy. These gifts show how we minister differently. The earlier metaphor of travel methods reminds us to grow spiritually in all ways.

But we should all grow in our faith, maturity, and character, things which provide the shared foundation for our different ministries. Ephesians 4:15 tells us, "We will grow to become *in every respect* the mature body of him who is the head, that is, Christ" . Or we don't develop spiritual maturity by just using a metaphorical motorcycle or a train or a plane or walking shoes. We need each aspect of spiritual maturity so we can be effective in ministry and arrive at our destination as we should.

So finally, how do we grow "in every respect"? I like the progression given by the apostle Peter: "Make every effort to add to your faith goodness; and to goodness, knowledge; and to knowledge, self-control; and to self-control, perseverance; and to perseverance, godliness; and to godliness, mutual affection; and to mutual affection, love. For if you possess *these* [eight different] *qualities in increasing measure, they will keep you from being ineffective* and unproductive in your knowledge of our Lord Jesus Christ" (2 Peter 1:5–8).

Maybe think of these eight different qualities in the sense of the various modes a traveler can use to become multidimensional. Yes, we should all travel in faith, goodness, knowledge, self-control, perseverance, godliness, mutual affection, and love.

Balance. I remember a financial advisor telling me to not put all my investment eggs in one basket, but to diversify. Maybe we should do the same spiritually, with the overall goal of growing up into Jesus by including all the measures. The result would be a breadth that helps us stand against storms and false teaching. The varied tools help us grow in every aspect. Not just some.

Kick-Starting the Application

Do you tend to have one area you stress to the detriment of others? Why might you stress or avoid one? Do you sense you may have neglected a more balanced approach to growing spiritually? Ask God to show you how you can broaden your base and begin with a new area—this week.

PS—If you're an author and could use a great publicist, I highly recommend Don Otis. Here's his site: https://www.veritasincorporated.com.

15—STRANGE DESTINATIONS

Early on a cold, rainy, and foggy morning, Rich rode his Harley Sportster and I my Honda Goldwing from Stewart, British Columbia, over the bridge into the thriving metropolis of Hyder, Alaska. Population 87 in 2010, down to 47 within 10 years. Others said 14. Even at the peak of its gold and silver mining dating back into the late 1890s, Hyder reached a grand total of just 250 people.

A strange American city that uses Canadian money. When you need law enforcement, you call the Royal Canadian Mounted Police. Hyder uses a Canadian energy provider, the kids attend Canadian schools, and it doesn't even use the Alaskan 907 area code, but the British Columbia one.

Locals call it "Alaska's Friendliest Ghost Town," but we saw no locals at 7 a.m. The drizzle and fog certainly gave it the look and feel of a ghost town with all details hazy—the moody half-light of Main Street made it feel even spookier.

Going to Hyder has one nice feature that comes with a kicker: travelers need no passports to enter Hyder, Alaska, from Stewart, British Columbia ... but they do to come back to Stewart. At the border checkpoint, Rich had misplaced his passport, couldn't find it for a while, and feared he might never see his wife again. I couldn't avoid softly singing the

Eagles's "Hotel California" to him, about how you get in free but it costs to get out. That didn't help him much at all.

Honestly, Hyder does seem like a strange vacation destination, but it was a logical one for me. I had a bit of an obsession to ride my motorcycle in all 50 states. My long ride back in 1974 had captured 31, which got me in the concert hall. By this point, I had bagged 46 and even got Hawaii while on a vacation. I begged a cooperative Harley dealer in Lihue, Kauai, for a test ride for one block. Just the summer before in Minnesota, we met some Pennsylvania bikers who mentioned Hyder is the southernmost Alaska town you can ride to, so that put Alaska close enough to be doable. Then in 2022, Jerry and I scored my last three—Florida, Georgia, and South Carolina.

The Hyder trip provides a number of takeaways. For fellow bikers and other nature enthusiasts, the 40 miles on 37A from Meziadin Junction in British Columbia to Stewart has made my top-four list. Glaciers on the south side and abundant waterfalls on the north make a narrow canyon with grizzly and brown bears, moose, deer, and other wildlife that will entice all who enjoy creation.

You'll cruise back decades or more. Maybe not close to the days of creation—the mountains continue to form and change from their creation but remain mostly untouched. A rough logging camp, Meziadin Junction provides the only gas and food for miles. Mankind has changed this wilderness only slightly—this country still has its fur on. And getting there, the route spanning Prince George to Meziadin exposes you to yet a different world of plains, farms, and logging. I guarantee you'll enjoy it all.

But a greater takeaway comes from insights about following and serving Jesus. Hyder suggests we expect some strange destinations and unexpected steps. While on his third missionary journey about 57 AD, Paul addressed the church in Rome—one of the rare places he hadn't yet visited, Rome lay strategically at the heart of the Roman Empire. He wrote, "I pray that ... the way may be opened for me to come to you. I long to see you ... I planned many times to come to you ... eager to preach the gospel also to you" (Romans 1:10–11, 13, 15).

For Paul, Rome was certainly not a strange destination, but his journey definitely was, considering the transportation method and stops along the way. Acts 26–28 tell the story. Instead of Paul going online with Uber and VRBO, the authorities in Jerusalem gave him an all-expense-paid cruise to Rome: in chains (26:30–32).

On that not-quite-luxury cruise, a storm struck: "The ship struck a sandbar and ran aground. The bow stuck fast and would not move, and the stern was broken to pieces by the pounding of the surf. The soldiers planned to kill the prisoners to prevent any of them from swimming away and escaping" (27:41–42). Scary news for the prisoners, until the soldiers changed their minds on killing them. But then Paul himself later faced another danger: "Paul gathered a pile of brushwood and, as he put it on the fire, a viper, driven out by the heat, fastened itself on his hand" (28:3).

Paul had a fine goal to extend the gospel but endured strange and unexpected steps in getting there. I suspect God has similar journeys for us, and we must factor some "strange and unexpected steps" into our expectations.

My life includes many unexpected steps. Not long after I returned to Christ, a church hired me as youth pastor, but within a year, they fired me. My response? If that's ministry, I'd rather drive a truck. Yeah, God provided an unsolicited job doing just that. I'd led a mission group two summers to a small village outside Taos, and in a string of nine coincidentally impossible events, God led me to a paying job living in a log cabin at a guest ranch in the mountains above Taos and to a church that healed me—ministry-wise.

But God and some in the church kept gently hinting I should be in ministry, so I finally left my almost-heaven Taos for a church in Lawndale, California, which has a 50 percent transiency rate. Top five in gang activity for all of SoCal. It was another strange destination for me. But there I met my wife, and that church set the foundation for more pastoring and writing. Strange, but welcome. God knows his stuff.

Expect some strange destinations and unusual stops along the way. Just walk with him.

KICK-STARTING THE APPLICATION

Think back to some strange places you've encountered, like the semi ghost town of Hyder. Did you expect those? How many times did God lead you to a strange destination? How did you respond to it? How did God reveal himself? What expectations might you have in thinking life is a full-on luxury cruise? Have those expectations helped you? How can you craft more biblical expectations?

16—START HARD

Back in 2018, at the age of 70, I attempted an Iron Butt ride, over 1,000 miles on two wheels in under 24 hours. Why? When younger, I had low self-confidence, and competing with others seemed to help. Upon coming to Christ, I realized he gave me enough value I had no need to compete with others, yet competition remained—with myself. I'd easily done an Iron Butt ride at 28 and wondered if, over four decades later, my toughness and determination remained. That question proved irresistible to this old fart.

The plan: jump on I-15 in Temecula, California, and head north 1,080 miles to Dillon, Montana.

Two teachers gave us insightful lessons. King Solomon wisely said, "We can make our plans, but the LORD determines our steps" (Proverbs 16:9 NLT). In other words, we act wisely when we plan. So I planned each gas and food stop.

Then Edward Murphy gave us the adage now known as Murphy's Law: "If anything can go wrong, it will." To that I add, "in the worst way at the worst time." So, those plans for each gas or food stop had margin for unexpected obstacles.

At 4 a.m., I fired up the Honda ST1300 and jumped on I-15 in darkness, with a hot cup of coffee in its holder. Just short of Barstow, I felt the driver's backrest slip loose; the cold weather gear bag was attached to it. A short stop fixed it, and I pulled into Las Vegas at 8:30, ahead of schedule, 273 miles down. But 40 miles north, that backrest slipped again, and the bag fell off. I did a quick brake as it had landed 100 yards back in the middle of the lane. I clumped along in my cowboy boots, then when I was 25 feet away, a truck ran over it. He seemed to aim.

Luckily, the gear was soft, but it took time to grab it and redesign the attachment. I arrived in Cedar City at 10:30, 460 miles down, almost halfway, but the miles and speed tired me more than anticipated. So I took an earlier-than-planned lunch at an old train station. Even so, I felt good about finishing. About 600 miles left but with over nine hours remaining.

For the next leg, I anticipated 210 miles to Provo, but Murphy struck again with tiredness, so I stopped early at Santaquin after 180 miles, with just 430 remaining.

The first lesson in counting the cost: figure out the hardest part and do it first. Solomon and Murphy make a wise team—I put margin in my schedule. The first 650 miles took just over nine hours, including stops, averaging almost 70 mph. Now to cover my butt legally, the speed limit here was 80, and traffic moved well above that. Going 430 miles in the remaining eight hours meant averaging only 54 mph. I relaxed. This was doable, short of a mechanical or human failure. I kept up the pace to shorten the time, but starting hard allowed me to take more and longer stops than the plan called for.

At 8:20 p.m. (my body clock, but Montana time was 9:20), I pulled into the Motel 6 in Dillon alive, needing a hot shower and a soft bed. Mission accomplished—ahead of schedule—but only because of planning well, leaving margin, and starting hard.

Those three reasons helped make my Iron Butt ride successful, and they also correspond with following Jesus.

First, let's plan our spiritual journey with even more intention than I did the Iron Butt—our ride with him has much more value than any bike ride. Jesus wants us to plan, to have spiritual goals. How shall we serve him? How will he lead us? What spiritual dreams do we have?

In the extended passage of Luke 14:25–33, Jesus gave essential requirements to qualify as a disciple. One has great relevance here: "But don't begin [to follow me] until you *count the cost*. For who would begin construction of a building without first calculating the cost to see if there is enough money to finish it? Otherwise, you might complete only the foundation before running out of money, and then everyone would laugh at you" (vv. 28–29 NLT).

Any good plan comes with costs. Friendships. Worldly success. Some of our dreams. Our self-will. Not only before we begin, but at each step along the way, we must decide he is our Lord, not just our Savior. He's boss and worth the costs.

Second, following Murphy's Law, realize things can go south, and sometimes in a hurry. Few of my anticipated stops followed my plan, and neither did I think of a bag falling off. Spiritually, we may anticipate upcoming problems, but we can't see them all. Nor can we avoid God choosing to get in the way, finessing our plans. Remember Proverbs 16:9: "We can make our plans, but the Lord *determines our steps*." As we plan our spiritual journey, let's not book ourselves so tightly we leave little room for God. We can then adjust when obstacles arise.

Third, follow Jesus's pattern of addressing the hardest things first. Hitting the first 500 miles hard when I was fresh allowed me the ability to take more breaks. Jesus seems to work the same way: he confronts us with the most difficult issue we face. For Nicodemus, the teacher of Israel, he had to give up that preeminence and start over as a baby (John 3:1–10). For the rich young ruler interested in following Jesus, he had to sell all he had and give the money to the poor (Matthew 19:16–22). Nicodemus did; the young man did not. May we give him our most difficult issue.

For us, let's analyze what our highest cost would be and begin working on that first. Put these three together, and our spiritual Iron Butt ride will end well.

KICK-STARTING THE APPLICATION

In planning, how well do you compensate for difficulties? Do you tend to start with the easier tasks to build some confidence or with the more difficult ones? How well do you invite God into the planning? What is the most difficult issue for you in following Jesus?

17—70 ISN'T 28

You'll see some posts about my 2018 Iron Butt ride scattered throughout this book, revealing different aspects and lessons from those 1,080 miles in 16 hours from metro SoCal to mountains to desert to farmland to more mountains. My Honda ST1300 had no music, so the ride was silent along the mostly straight, sometimes barren, and sometimes scenic I-15 from Temecula, California, to Dillon, Montana.

More recently, my phone sits on its mount on my bikes, sometimes featuring Waze or classic rock, worship music, or Iz on Pandora, but mostly, it's turned off. I've lived on Simon & Garfunkel's old tune "The Sound of Silence." I cherish silence and prayer and pondering, especially outdoors. God and I have done a lot of business in the quiet, which has generated many posts for my website, *Unconventional*, two books, and influenced my entire life.

After leaving at 4 a.m. and traveling 460 miles, I entered Cedar City, Utah, at 10:30. I'd made good time but already felt tired. This longer-than-planned pit stop provided me an early lunch and rest and prompted a fresh topic for me to ponder—70 isn't 28. I hadn't fully anticipated the changes until that morning's ride.

While sipping on a coffee, my thoughts went to my first unintended Iron Butt at 28. Early in a foggy morning, I had pulled out of West Lafayette, Indiana, on a semi-chopped 750 Honda. I'd helped a good friend, John Southwood, get hitched, with various celebrations and pranks contributing to the festivities.

Eager to get home to my log cabin in the mountains of Taos, I flew, much of the time going 95 to 100 with only a few short stops, and I felt bulletproof as the odometer passed 1,000 miles. I just had one delay somewhere in Kansas to help a single woman driver being harassed by some guys in a car. The image of a longhaired biker on a chopper came in handy then. Somewhere south of Dodge City around midnight, the bike sputtered. The main tank was running dry, so I reached down to flip the reserve on, but I'd not reset it at the last stop—it was dry. I coasted to the tall grass on the roadside and spent the night there in my sleeping bag. Apart from the gas, I would have ridden farther. Now, I discovered my endurance then didn't match my experience at 70.

With a driver's backrest, the ST1300 was more comfortable and faster. It also featured a big tank that gave a great range between fill-ups, throttle locks, and a nice fairing with a windshield to block the blasts at 100 mph. It was a great bike for long rides. The route was nearly all empty and straight interstate, with a speed limit that reached 80.

On the first ride, the 750 had no windshield or fairing, no throttle lock, and no backrest. Also, just half the route was interstate, with most of it two-lane state highways. Yet I never grew tired. So, why was the second ride much more difficult? Well, 70 isn't 28. Changes occur.

But what tips on spiritual life came from my ponderings in that railroad station café on my second Iron Butt?

We must realize life changes. Age changed my second ride, and each decade brings new physical issues. Jobs change, for the good and bad, either with the same company or a new one. Relationships change, often daily. Family. Churches. Culture. And we need to not just realize it but accept it as a reality to respond to. We're better off choosing our responses to change rather than feeling like their victims.

Also, keep your primary goal to know and serve God. Jesus's admonition on the greatest commandment can serve as our North Star to keep us on track to our destination: "You must love the Lord your God with all your heart, all your soul, and all your mind" (Matthew 22:37 NLT). In all the changes that come, cling to this. Keep in mind, we grow in our knowledge of Scripture and faith, so let's remain open to flexing and changing on both what they are and how to do them. A refusal to change reveals a person is stuck, not continuing to learn, grow, and develop.

By nature, faith is dynamic and growing, and Peter gives us steps on how we target our primary goal through the changes we face.

> Make every effort to add to your faith goodness; and to goodness, knowledge; and to knowledge, self-control; and to self-control, perseverance; and to perseverance, godliness; and to godliness, mutual affection; and to mutual affection, love. For if you possess these qualities in increasing measure, they will keep you from being ineffective and unproductive in your knowledge of our Lord Jesus Christ. (2 Peter 1:5–8)

Make your plans to navigate change but hold them loosely and weave God into all. I love the message in James 4:13–16 NLT:

> Look here, you who say, "Today or tomorrow *we are* going to a certain town and will stay there a year. We will do business there and make a profit." How do you know what your life will be like tomorrow? *Your life is like the morning fog*—it's here a little while, then it's

gone. What you ought to say is, "*If the Lord* wants us to, we will live and do this or that." Otherwise you are boasting about your own pretentious plans, and all such boasting is evil .

Another thing I learned. While 70 may not equal 28, it doesn't mean decrepit. I survived the Iron Butt ride ... safely. And rode 220 miles the next morning before breakfast in Butte. Then in 2022, a friend and I did a 6,500 mile ride to East Coast ... but that's a story for another time.

Kick-Starting the Application

Think of some life changes you've enjoyed. What made them good? How can you use them as a foundation for future changes? Think of some changes you didn't appreciate. What made them negative? How did God work in them, or how could he have worked? What are some changes you can incorporate into following Jesus?

18—NO LONGER AN OUTSIDER

BY LIBBY TAYLOR, AUTHOR

Our first date was on a motorcycle. First we had lunch, then we stopped at a tattoo parlor to pay respects to the owner, who was also the president of an outlaw motorcycle club. Other women might consider this a one-and-done date, but Wayne intrigued me. He desired to advance God's kingdom by living a genuine, loving lifestyle of integrity that makes Christianity attractive to nonbelievers. We married a year later, with both motorcycle parking and a helmet and leather check (a hat check for bikers) at the church. Among the guest list, we had friends from three outlaw clubs, including two convicted murderers, one just out of San Quentin.

These types of guests were exactly what we'd discussed when planning the invitation list. I had come to know Jesus as a result of going to a wedding and wanted others who don't normally attend church to hear about Jesus.

Following our October wedding, we attended a holiday fair where one of the outlaw clubs hosted a food booth. After my husband ordered our meals, I made a point to say hello to those who'd attended our wedding. Their response, or should I say their lack of response, was disappointing. They didn't even acknowledge I had spoken.

I'd heard the outlaw culture was based on loyalty and trust, despite the fact they had a different set of values than mine. Now, I was forced to admit they didn't trust me. They knew I was married to someone they trusted, but it was clear I had to earn *my own* trust. I had to demonstrate my own loyalty to prove I wasn't just in it to rack up brownie points with God.

In April, I attended a baby shower for the club president's wife. With her due date only weeks before Mother's Day, and since she'd had a difficult pregnancy, I included an early Mother's Day gift—a gift card to a specialty coffee shop. Also, I wrote a note recognizing the especially difficult time she'd endured as a soon-to-be mother.

That summer, a group of Christian riders attended this club's campout. I did kids' ministry, set up the s'mores for Saturday around the bonfire, and helped with the 24-hour coffee bar. The club president knew I was alone since Wayne was at the Memorial Day motorcycle rally in Washington, DC. He approached me expressly to say one thing: "We got your back." I was a bit surprised, not sure what he meant. He went on to say, "While Wayne's gone, if anyone gives you any trouble, any trouble at all, just call. We got your back."

Then I knew. I'd earned the highest level of camaraderie between an outlaw club and someone wearing a Christian patch. He'd offered help—like many others from my church and motorcycle ministry—but this was also an offer of protection. Having no fear for my safety, I simply replied, "Thank you."

Only then did I realize I'd finally earned their trust.

Three thoughts and a caution struck me from Libby's story, ones that can benefit and challenge all followers of

Jesus. First, Wayne desired to model a Christian faith that attracts those who don't follow Jesus. This desire drew Libby to him. Wayne and their wedding plans exemplify how we should all share our faith—with consistent intentionality. We craft our lives, our activities, like they did with their wedding, to let them know about Jesus.

Yes, we're all called to be intentional about our faith. With his last words before his ascension, Jesus gave us our mission: "I have been given all authority in heaven and on earth. *Therefore*, go and *make disciples* of all the nations, baptizing them in the name of the Father and the Son and the Holy Spirit. Teach these new disciples to obey all the commands I have given you" (Matthew 28:18–20 NLT).

Many of us take advantage of nice coincidences, but Libby and Wayne create intentional opportunities. Here's one example of mine that sometimes sparks good conversations. When a chance acquaintance asks me how I'm doing, I often respond, "Better than I deserve." Some ignore it and move on, so I do as well. But others ask about it, and I gently bring in grace, that I get better than I deserve. Some conversations go deep. Not all, but some.

Second, Libby and Wayne intentionally identified with and respected their target: outlaw bikers. Their key was living "a genuine, loving lifestyle of integrity." They didn't pretend to share life—they authentically did share life events and knew their culture. They didn't compromise their values or attack those they didn't agree with. They respected others' individuality enough to allow them to disagree.

Isn't that how Jesus lived? He became a man, sharing all our troubles. He only attacked the religious hypocritical leaders who gave God a bad name. Notice the term "loving lifestyle" Libby used. Didn't Jesus also say the second greatest command is loving our neighbors?

Third, they served and helped—the classic way of earning the right to be heard. Libby demonstrated this service at the baby shower and outlaw club's campout. Her actions sound suspiciously like Jesus's brother saying in James 2:18 that genuine faith produces godly behavior. Libby earned the right to be trusted by what she did.

But we need a caveat—a warning. When practicing these three concepts, we create an environment that enhances the chance others will accept Jesus, but we can't ensure it. God gives all people the ability to choose or not. All we have in our power is demonstrating a genuine life that "makes Christianity attractive to nonbelievers."

The choice is theirs, and we need to respect that, giving them the freedom to disagree. It's ironic how that freedom tends to help them choose faith. Our job, like Wayne and Libby demonstrated, is to give people a good choice. Intentionally.

Kick-Starting the Application

How intentional are you in bringing Jesus into conversations or encounters? What works best for you? Do you tend to push away those who don't live by your values or find a link to better connect? Do you have specific people you feel drawn to share Jesus with?

Libby Taylor is a freelance writer residing in Northern California with her husband, Wayne, and their "kids"—Abby, a chihuahua, and Cecil, an Amazon parrot. Wayne and Libby minister together through the Christian Motorcyclists Association. You can contact Libby at libbytw@wavecable.com.

19—BALANCING RISKS

Life. No one gets out alive—at least physically. We can choose a life of safety and stability and see little change, much like the moon only shows one side. If we do so, we grow slightly and contribute little to make the world better. Or we can decry safety for adventure, go out early in a meteor's blaze of glory, and likewise have merely a minor impact on our world. But most of us live in between, balancing safety, adventure, and impact. So, how do we maximize the time we have in a manner that makes God smile at our impact? We must keep in mind the purpose we choose for our lives. This poem expresses the tension between safety and adventure (all poems in the book are mine).

Balanced Risks

Ron rode safely
    at his wife's demand
    full-face helmet
        insulated from the smells and wind in his
   face
    full body armor in jacket and pants
        walking like Iron Man
    gauntlet gloves
        in a SoCal August
sweat dripped down his face

when we stopped for gas
he tried to smile
> claiming he loved to ride
> yet rode just a year
> sold his bike at a loss
> the drive for safety draining the joy of riding

Cal used his crotch rocket
> as the engineers designed
> a powerful bike that nearly flew
> Levi's and a T-shirt and half helmet
> bragging at the bar
> about breaking 150
>> on a curvy Sierra mountain road

later, a smile graced his face
> as he pushed it to 160
>> until he hit a small pebble
> and tumbled and finally flew and hugged a tree

I saw him two years later
limping with one decent leg
> a limp arm at his side
> as he loaded another crashed bike
>> onto the bed of his tow truck
> grimacing in unspoken pain

shamefully telling us how
> he used to ride

Yet I ride

Earlier, I had Honda's ST1300, and I rode it to match the sport-touring bike it was. Its acceleration and cornering balance amazed me, and I scraped pegs more than once. Not many passed me on the twisties, and no one in my riding groups pulled away from me. And truly, I rode as worship, enjoying the intersection of God's creation, physical laws, and human ingenuity that could craft such a vehicle. Riding would never take the place of gathered worship, but it certainly supplemented it. And riding does increase my prayer life.

Then at about 71, my balance and reactions slowed down, and the risk increased with the ST. I don't think I could have ridden slow on it, and a major injury or death wouldn't have been fair to my wife and would have ended any chance for touching others for Jesus. So I balanced my love of fast riding with my new normal and transitioned to the less tempting Goldwing. It had plenty of power, nice cornering, and great comfort but was not a sport bike. So still I ride—more wisely. Balancing risk. Adjusting.

Paul the apostle traveled the world to tell people about Jesus, taking risks and never backing off. Sometimes left for dead. Sometimes sneaking out of town in the dark to stay alive, rather than remaining in the town as a further target. Balancing risks. True to his calling, taking risks to do it, yet wisely doing what he could to continue. We share a major trait with Paul—a command to work for God's kingdom.

God doesn't call us all to go to Africa or Vietnam as missionaries or to pastoral ministry. But we all minister to build his church: "So Christ himself gave the apostles, the prophets, the evangelists, the pastors and teachers, to equip his people for *works of service*, so that the body of Christ may be built up" (Ephesians 4:11–12. The word *service* often gets translated as *ministry*.

So, a quick question: how do we balance our lives to be the most useful to God? Yes, we take care of our and our family's needs. Yes, we need leisure and recreation time. Yes, we can take some risks in our adventures. But do we purposefully balance our desires for risk or safety with our ministry of impacting others for Jesus? Folks, according to that passage in Ephesians, following Jesus means we share in his job of building his church.

I recently studied Paul's partner Onesimus, and discovered his name means *useful*, which led me to examine our usefulness to God. How useful are we to God with our gifts and talents? First Peter 4:10–11 says, "Each of you should use whatever gift you have received to serve others ... If anyone speaks, they should do so as one who speaks the very words of God. If anyone serves, they should do it with the strength God provides, so that in all things God may be praised through Jesus."

How useful are we with our material goods? Jesus began telling this parable to his disciples: "There was a rich man whose manager was accused of wasting his possessions" (Luke 16:1). God gives us the use of material things but retains ownership, and we give account to him on how we used them. Do we use them for kingdom purposes along with our needs?

How useful are we with our faith, our words about Jesus? In Ezekiel 33, God tells his people they are watchmen, to let others know of their need for God. Do we spread grace with our words or act as secret agents for God?

Are we willing to risk to serve God and/or enjoy life? How much? How do we calculate the risk-reward ratio? I have no set answers for you, just an encouragement to think about this question. Pray about this. Maybe you need to increase your risks. Maybe decrease them. But I suspect, as you ponder this chapter, you'll start to come to grips with your priorities. Have fun in the process!

KICK-STARTING THE APPLICATION

Do you lean risk-averse or risk-embracing? Have you deliberately examined what risks you choose or reject, taking God into account? How does your level of risk factor into being useful to God? What priorities seem to emerge as you consider balancing risks?

20—TRY SOME ROAD KINDNESS

Our Gray Hogs group planned a route crisscrossing California's Sierra Nevada mountains, starting at the south going north, and east to west and back and back and ... I'd found a website for motorcycles and the passes, and we planned to hit the major ones. Our first entry came at Sequoia National Park on Highway 198 by Exeter, and then we split up a bit. The south entry had a lot of very sharp turns, which would tire Mick and made Jerry leery on his three-wheeled Can Am. So they took the shorter and smoother J21 north, while Brad and I hit Highway 198 east, then north, then west in a nice loop.

That route gave us delightful riding, and the curves matched the map ... tight. Brad and I worked our way ahead of the slight traffic, pulled over for a break, and strolled through the redwoods over to the General Sherman Tree, and hopped back on heading for the north exit. We quickly caught up to a very slow-moving pickup towing a very big trailer, with solid double lines on the road meaning DON'T PASS. We obeyed.

Yeah, we got frustrated a little at the pace, but the driver kindly took the first chance at a turnout, and our bikes became bikes again. As we carved the turns, I pondered the goodness of receiving kindness. Frankly, a lot of slow drivers seem oblivious to holding up the vehicles following them. And yes, some of these sport Christian symbols of varied versions. Maybe they bought the cars used?

Yet an event two days later demonstrated kindness is a double-edged sword. If we appreciate receiving it, we should also dispense it. After Sequoia, we spent the night in Fresno and took Highway 168 north to Yosemite to hit the famed Tioga Pass, Highway 120. We took it slow to sightsee, stopping a lot for the scenery and pics. Tioga deserves its reputation. Most of the time Brad led, our wizard of Waze, followed by Mick, me, and Jerry riding drag.

Dinner came at the well-known Whoa Nellie Deli in Lee Vining, then we jumped on 395 to Bridgeport, our destination for the night. But this time, Mick followed me. After parking our bikes, Mick mentioned my back tire was pretty worn. I doubted him at first because I'd checked them before we left, but he knew his tires—the threads were showing. I called around and found a shop 60 miles north in Carson Valley, Nevada. They had the tire in stock and could fit me in the next morning.

Mick and Brad took some other routes to meet us there, so Jerry and I went north. I usually like to go fast, but the tire scared me, so I crawled up 395 at 55 mph to Carson Valley, praying often. Going 10 below the limit caused a lot of cars to back up, and I remembered the kindness of the pickup/trailer driver two days earlier. So, at the first chance I pulled over for 10 cars. Soon I did another pullover, for 20 this time. Frankly, the nice feeling at giving kindness was just as good as receiving it earlier. Maybe better. Honest.

My lesson: kindness works—both in giving and receiving. Not surprisingly, it's part of the fruit of the Spirit. And while giving kindness in this age of road rage is both rare and right, kindness should touch every arena of life. Marriages. Work. Neighbors. Perhaps even politics?

But what's the essence and importance of kindness? The original Greek word for *kindness* in the fruit in Ephesians 5:22 gets translated as gentleness, goodness, excellence, or that we work well with people without bitterness or harshness. As a fruit of the Spirit, it flows from the character of God. Now, here come some scary thoughts about his kindness.

Luke 6:35 tells us, "But love your enemies, do good to them ... Then your reward will be great, and you will be children of the Most High, because *he is kind to the ungrateful and wicked.*" This verse reveals the difference between doing some kind things and being a kind person: kind people consistently follow God's example in showing kindness to all, even the wicked, like God does. So, how do we express kindness biblically?

In Acts 3–4, Peter and John healed a crippled beggar, and some religious leaders objected. Peter described what they had done as "an *act of kindness* shown to a man who was lame" (Acts 4:9). When we help meet the needs of people when we can, we demonstrate God's kindness lives in us. Kindness helps those in need.

Kindness also comes out in our language, something sorely needed in our fractured times. Paul writes, "When we are cursed, we bless; when we are persecuted, we endure it; when we are slandered, *we answer kindly*" (1 Corinthians 4:12–13). Even when others disagree with us, or even slander us, we respond with kindness. Those situations really require another facet of the fruit—self-control. We pause before responding to seek the kind answer.

Kindness improves relationships: "Be kind and compassionate to one another, forgiving each other, just as in Christ God forgave you" (Ephesians 4:32). Kindness connects to compassion, feeling with others, and forgiving each other. Try to imagine how relationships would improve if we kindly forgave, kindly ended grudges, and kindly resolved issues.

Isn't that what Jesus meant when he gave the Golden Rule (Luke 6:31), to treat others as we'd like to be? I tend to want justice when I'm wronged. But when I wrong someone, I yearn for grace. For kindness.

I suspect we all enjoy receiving grace gifts of kindness, but let's remember kindness is a two-way street. As we forgive, so shall we be forgiven.

Kick-Starting the Application

What most convicts you about this chapter? What most encourages you? If you asked friends and family to rate you using a scale of one to ten on being a kindness giver, how would you rank? Would you be happy with your score? Is God likely to be happy with your score? Commit to two acts of kindness this week and ponder their impact on you and the receiver.

21—PATIENCE PAYS OFF

Our Gray Hogs' 2021 ride through the Sierras had an unusual end—for several reasons. Brad was leading the four of us through the city traffic of Auburn back to our hotel. He took a quick look back to see we all could make the left turn, and a minivan halted directly in front of him. He hit the brakes and tried to swerve but still collided with the minivan and tumbled to the street. He was shaken up, bruised, and had sore muscles, but suffered no major damage to him—just to his Goldwing, which was totaled. His son came over the next morning from Nevada to drive him home to Long Beach, California.

That night, we four sat in the hotel restaurant talking, laughing, and reminiscing. Brad said this would be his last ride. He would soon be moving to northern Idaho, with too much snow and cold to ride road bikes for much of the year, so he wasn't going to replace the totaled bike. Mick, at 82, said it was finally time to call it a day for riding. He'd quit once before, but after a year he missed it too much. He would stick to it this time. This turned out to be the last supper for the core four of the Gray Hogs.

But the endings hadn't ended quite yet. While at the table, Jerry realized he had to get home to Keizer, Oregon, soon, which he often did. Funny how the trip and its length had been planned for nearly a year, but once he smelled the pines that reminded him of Oregon, he took off early for home the next morning.

That left just Mick and me heading east over the Sierras to see his daughter and son-in-law in Susanville for a family gathering for two nights before heading home ourselves to SoCal. The first morning, Mick suggested he and I ride for breakfast to a cool café in Chester, about 35 miles west. A fine ride through mountains and meadows and a lake and regrowing burn areas from the big fire the year before. We found the Cravings Café and sat down outside for breakfast. A great way to start a day, a nice ride and an outside café.

Right behind Mick's seat was an espaliered apple tree. Espaliering just means the gardener trained it to grow on a flat surface or trellis by pruning to get a strong vertical central stem, then pruning the branches to grow horizontally side to side or in a geometric pattern. This method provides fruit without the tree taking up much three-dimensional space.[1] It might have been a foot from the front to the back of the tree.

Espaliering requires a lot of work and time—tying up the branches to a trellis or wires so they grow properly, pruning branches that don't follow the pattern, and waiting. Mick could have reached back and grabbed an apple ... but they hadn't ripened yet.

And seeing the espaliered tree taught me a lesson about myself—and maybe you're similar. Typically, I want what I want and when I want it. Delayed gratification may be a mark of maturity, but it doesn't come naturally for me. Yes, delay can ruin some opportunities—I get that. And some things come to pass, not to stay. But some good things that come to stay, like espaliering a tree, take time, and we shouldn't give up too soon. Growing into godliness would be one of them.

In Galatians, Paul gives several tips on how to become more Christlike, more mature spiritually. A pretty wise guy, he realized growth is a battle where we face obstacles, so he gave us encouragement that patience pays off: "Let us not become weary in doing good, for at the proper time *we will reap a harvest if we do not give up*" (Galatians 6:9). If we get tired and think of quitting when we should carry on, patience can get us through.

So, just what is patience? I almost apologize, but the literal meaning in the original Greek is *long-suffering*. We continue despite all the obstacles in our path and the difficulties they bring. Very simply, like the verse from Galatians says, patience means we do not give up. We use self-restraint in the face of provocation. We don't instinctively retaliate, which focuses on our anger because patience is the opposite of quick-tempered. Even if we have a valid reason to take vengeance, we don't. We pause enough to consider a godly response.

Patience also means we don't surrender to difficult circumstances. We don't quit when life or the task gets hard. We don't give in to despair when we see no path to the desired end. Frankly, not giving up doesn't match our nature, does it? We need some supernatural strength, the strength we gain from knowing Jesus and having him live in us, like 1 Timothy 1:16 says: "But for that very reason I was shown mercy so that in me, the worst of sinners, Christ Jesus might display *his immense patience* as an example for those who would believe on him and receive eternal life."

God restrains himself when we should be Post Toasties because patience permeates his character. We love others, not through our love, but with the love God has for others. In the same manner, may we be patient toward others and ourselves and our mission through the unlimited patience of the Jesus who lives in us.

Let's not grow tired of the struggle. It will bring good results. In time. And maybe we can grow, like that espaliered apple tree, and provide good fruit.

KICK-STARTING THE APPLICATION

In what areas do you struggle with patience? Can you sense if your struggle is a holy dissatisfaction of God closing a door, or just impatience or being tired on your part? Are there some specific areas you find it hard to be patient in? Any ideas why? Earlier in Galatians, Paul said one fruit of the Spirit is patience. How are you nurturing that fruit?

22—VARIETY & DIFFERENCES

The Gray Hogs ride of 2021 had several unexpected twists at the end. The plan had Mick and Brad riding from Grass Valley on the western slope of the Sierra in Northern California to Susanville on the east side for a family celebration, and Jerry and I would ride more in the western Sierra. But then the Scottish poet Robert Burns stepped in with his line, "The best-laid schemes of mice and men often get screwed up ..." Well, I may have adapted that thought somewhat.

But within five miles of our hotel to end Wednesday's ride, Brad and a car collided, totaling his Goldwing that looked almost new. He had some bruises and some very sore muscles but nothing broken. Even so, that accident ended the trip for him. The next morning, his son drove over from Nevada to get Brad and his gear back to SoCal, and Jerry decided he'd head home early to Oregon. Yes, that is typical for Jerry.

That left Mick at 80 to ride alone the 180 miles across the spine of the Sierra to Susanville and 580 more down to his home in Long Beach. No doubt at all he could make it, but it's generally safer to ride with another, so I told him I'd go along. And in part, it was an excuse to ride more in the mountains.

So on Thursday, Mick and I dropped south a little from Grass Valley to catch the quickest route, I-80 to Reno, then 395 north to Susanville. Interstate 80 is a wide freeway right through the beautiful heart of the Sierra. Our biggest issue was not getting stuck on the ruts made by the large semis on a road troubled by snow and ice. Well, rubbernecking at the beauty came in a close second on the danger scale.

We arrived safely in Susanville that afternoon, and since Friday afternoon was the family celebration, I gave them some private time. I took off on a solo ride north on Highway 139 past Eagle Lake to Alturas. Alturas has a country café with some of the best cinnamon rolls I've had, and my body forces me to stop if I'm within 20 miles of it. After lunch, the bike turned south on Highway 395 back to Susanville. That overall ride provided me 135 miles of pure bliss to enjoy the scenery of majestic mountains, lush grassy meadows, high desert, good-sized lakes, and dry creek beds. Ponderosa pines and aspen and cedar and pinyon pines. Deer and cattle and eagles and hawks and juncos and who knows what else.

I left the phone and its music in the fairing pocket to enhance some fine times of meditation and prayer. I wrote this chapter from what God whispered to me that day.

Clearly, he placed an abundance of variety in our world. Different, but all aspects of the terrain work together. All aspects of plant and animal life work together. The thought struck me, stealing a line from Mark Twain about common people: God must love variety—he made so much of it.

The silence and meditation caused a deeper thought to hit my slow mind. After each day of creating the physical world, he pronounced it good.

I tend to see deserts as a lot of barren ground to cover before reaching the mountains and their forests. Yet God called them good. I didn't understand his reasons, so I did some research about what deserts contribute. They provide us with the easy extraction of numerous essential minerals, not to mention over 50 percent of the earth's copper.[1] Don't forget those solar and wind farms as we quickly ride through deserts.

The mountains grace us with more than their beauty—they give us fresh, clean water. In fact, mountains can be thought of as the earth's "water towers," contributing most of its freshwater supply.[2] And their trees turn carbon dioxide into oxygen, helping minimize the impact of climate change.

Okay, how about the valleys? Their rich soil feeds us, and their rivers bring water from the mountains down to us. Considering all that every part of creation provides, maybe I should better love and appreciate all of it.

But the true lesson goes deeper, so let's back up. On the sixth day, God made humans and pronounced it very good. So, do we pronounce people as good?

I tend to spend little time with those who don't share my beliefs and values and behaviors. They are the deserts I rush by. Why can't I love and extend grace and companionship to those who differ from me? Why can't I cherish everyone as God does? After all, he gave his Son, Jesus, for all the people in the world. I suspect God's love isn't limited to those who agree with him ... because none of us fully do.

When asked about the most important commandment, Jesus answered,

> "'Love the LORD your God with all your heart and with all your soul and with all your mind.' This is the first and greatest commandment. And the second is like it: 'Love your neighbor as yourself.' All the Law and the Prophets hang on these two commandments." (Matthew 22:37–40)

Notice implications of that last sentence, because we do nothing out of love for God unless we also love our neighbor. And remember, Jesus defined our neighbor as anyone we come into contact with who has a need (Luke 10:29–37)—a pretty broad definition.

And maybe, just maybe, I need to give a special measure of God's love and grace to those who don't agree with me, to those with different backgrounds or cultures, to those I don't feel comfortable around. Obviously, showing love and acceptance doesn't mean we agree with them, but we value them to the same measure God does. Maybe then they might listen to us with respect, if we begin by listening to them with respect?

A high challenge? Yep. But can we justify not striving to treat different people as God treats us? I think not.

KICK-STARTING THE APPLICATION

Think about your interactions, either in person, on social media, or even on broadcast media. Would an unbiased observer consistently see love and respect in how you disagree with others? If not, should you change? What changes could you make? Will you?

23—LIFE LESSONS

BY JERRY CHRISTENSEN (ONE OF THE ORIGINAL GRAY HOGS), RETIRED PASTOR, BIKER

How you approach life really makes a difference. If you've followed Tim on his motorcycle adventures, then you've probably heard him refer to me. I'm the guy in 2022 who didn't get to finish riding my motorcycle in all 50 states. Oh, we came close, but no cigars. With my bike going on the fritz and Tim getting in a wreck, that dream came to an abrupt end.

So in 2023, we tried again, but my back and leg pain kicked in and once more shattered that dream, so we decided on a week of riding in Northern California. On the first day, I got up early and headed out. Everything was going great. I stopped at my favorite restaurant in Grants Pass and had my usual Long John Silver's Chicken Planks and crumbs; it really doesn't get much better than that.

After lunch, I continued heading south for Medford to find my motel. In my experience, most motels are near the freeway, so I entered the address and followed the directions. But when I reached the exit, Waze had me going about five miles east, then another few miles south, and then a couple of miles back west ... the route was ridiculous.

When I finally arrived, I really had no idea where I was. But while loading the bike in the morning, I started talking to a fellow traveler and found out I was only about a mile to the freeway, certainly nothing to be upset about. Apparently Waze thought that going 10 miles out of my way was faster than going south a few more miles and then west two miles.

And while in the big picture this roundabout route really wasn't a big problem, it wasn't what I expected and made no sense. But life is like that, isn't it? Sometimes things go as planned, and sometimes we have to go 10 miles out of our way. When the latter happens, we can choose to get all upset, or to take a few deep breaths and go with the flow. I decided to choose the latter, which gave me a much better ending to an otherwise great day of riding. Why? I remembered some lines from Ecclesiastes:

> There is a time for everything,
>   and a season for every activity under the heavens ...
> a time to mourn and a time to dance. (3:1, 4)

And while my little detour was certainly a small thing, I still had to decide how I was going to respond. Thankfully, rolling with the punches made the beginning of a great trip something to laugh at.

How we deal with life's curves matters. I think the writer of Ecclesiastes was spot on. While there is certainly a time to weep and mourn, there is also a time to laugh and dance. I decided to laugh, but at 76, I chose not to dance.

Jerry's memory of that Ecclesiastes passage shows a deep truth many of us battle with, and I'm at the top of the list. When things don't go according to plan, like Jerry's detour that made no sense, we choose one of two options:

to mourn and get ticked off and angry, or to laugh in the face of the trouble ... and maybe do a dance step or two. I suggest the response we choose both reveals our inner person and sets us up for character traits that last.

Here's why. In earlier years, I got upset at the bad I experienced and saw and became pessimistic, seeing a gloomy future. I even wondered if life was worth living. I was not a fun person to be around, and I seriously contemplated suicide—I saw no light in my future. Then I came across a passage that saved my life: "Finally, brothers and sisters, whatever is true, whatever is noble, whatever is right, whatever is pure, whatever is lovely, whatever is admirable—if anything is excellent or praiseworthy—*think about such things*. Whatever you have learned or received or heard from me, or seen in me—put it into practice. *And the God of peace will be with you*" (Philippians 4:8–9).

I started obeying these verses. When things went south, I replaced my normally negative thoughts with positive ones: "God, you've got me out of this before. I know you can again." Or if a temptation hit hard that I'd given into before, I'd think, "God, thank you I'm not that person anymore."

I began to get confidence in the process and sensed God's peace growing in me. I chose to start focusing on the positive, and my change in focus built a trait of optimism not natural for me. Negative thoughts still come in, but I try to quickly replace them with ones that match those eight traits in the Philippians passage. I appreciate this new me, so contradictory to my earlier self. When I focused on darkness, darkness grew. When I focused on light, light grew.

We cannot control all the things that impact our lives. But we can choose to laugh and dance.

And Jerry's story brings another lesson. I loved how Waze took him way out of his way, either because of traffic, an accident, or the closest off-ramp being closed. And the next morning, Waze didn't send him backtracking, but to a closer ramp. Why did that Ecclesiastes passage pop into his mind? He'd spent a lifetime in God's Word, and that relevant verse was there. Doesn't God's Word work better than Waze?

> Your word is a lamp to my feet,
>   a light on my path.
> I have taken an oath and confirmed it,
>   that I will follow your righteous laws.
> (Psalm 119:105–106)

Get to know and value God's Word as showing the best way to go.

Kick-Starting the Application

What is typically your first response when annoying things happen? What role does God play there? Have you tried the hack of replacing a negative thought with a positive one?

Jerry Christensen was born in Long Beach, California, a long time ago and later, became a pastor, serving churches in Oregon, New Mexico, Oklahoma, and California. His love of riding motorcycles began at around 10 years old, riding Cushman scooters on his aunt and uncle's grape farm. He's put a lot of miles on around 20 different bikes and still rides as often as the Oregon weather allows.

24—OFFER HELP

The British Columbia coast can be chilly, cloudy, and wet, even in the summer, and the cold bit deep that day as we hopped onto the ferry in Port Angeles, Washington, heading to Victoria on Vancouver Island. Then we rode north to catch the Nanaimo ferry, crossing the ocean again to reach Vancouver, British Columbia. Mick, a fellow lover of coffee, spotted a Tim Horton's restaurant, which put smiles on all our faces. We parked our six bikes, walked inside, ordered coffee and pastries, and waited for the life-giving warmth the coffee would produce in our bodies. When the waitress brought the cups, our first step was grabbing them to warm our hands. Then came the drinking to warm our insides. Multitasking.

Yet we'd barely taken our first sip when we saw four guys, all dressed in biker gear, walk across the street into the parking lot, take some brief looks at our bikes, only to enter Tim's, look around, then walk to our table. Four smiles, and one spoke: "The helmets give you away. You guys must belong to those bikes outside. We saw your plates from the States, and you're the only ones here with helmets. Our bikes are on the other side of the street. Welcome to Canada! Can we help you in any way?"

We invited them to join us, and we shared coffee. Well, some drank tea (remember, this was Canada). We talked about our bikes and how we'd met some Canadian bikers two years before in Grangeville, Idaho. The bikers we were sitting with preferred riding in the States, which I didn't understand—British Columbia and Alberta have some stunning rides. They gave us some ideas of where to ride, what to avoid. They asked us to ride with them that day, but we were enroute to Whistler on Highway 99 and asked them to join us, but they all had to show up for work the next day.

In part, our chance meeting with them was the brotherhood of the road, bikers connecting with bikers. We had four Goldwings, one from 1978, and the other three just four years old, a Harley Sportster, and an older Honda 750. We came from Oregon, California, and South Dakota. Their bikes were also varied, a Victory and several smaller bikes, as best I recall, but all were from British Columbia. Beyond us sharing the biking life, our connection was enhanced by their hospitality as four Canadian locals.

My first trip in 1970 took me to Canada, and our group has ridden in Canada frequently over the years. We've always found the folks to be exceptionally friendly, but this meeting even exceeded our previous experiences. We talked for days about their great example of hospitality, which has now made its way onto the pages of this book. The Canadians have a knack for hospitality we all could learn from.

And about every time I remember this story, a passage comes to mind that challenges me to the root of my being: "Keep on loving one another as brothers and sisters. Do not forget to *show hospitality to strangers*, for by so doing some people have shown *hospitality to angels without knowing it*. Continue to remember those in prison, as if you were together with them in prison, and those who are mistreated *as if you yourselves* were suffering" (Hebrews 13:1–3).

For those of us who follow Jesus, who desire to become more like him, active hospitality should denote our lives.

We recognize mutual love, or action to benefit the other, is part of what Jesus proclaimed as the greatest commandments. One expression of love is to show hospitality to strangers, like the Canadian bikers did for us. I have no clue if they thought we might be angels, but I can confirm none of us are. At times, I wonder if they were angels, giving us an example of how to behave. I need those reminders.

I just recently noticed something after the command to show hospitality to strangers, to those in prison, to those who are mistreated—and we can expand that circle to anyone in dire straits. The verse continues with the words "as if you yourselves were suffering." The writer of Hebrews knew his stuff and put that phrase there for a reason—it reveals a great tactic on showing hospitality: empathy. Some call it sympathy, literally meaning to share the feelings of another, although some mistake sympathy for feeling sorry for someone. Empathy isn't feeling the same thing as another; it's feeling with them. It's a close meaning but significantly different.

Empathy may not include sharing the same feelings, but it strives to understand the feelings of another even if we don't share them. As if we put ourselves in their shoes. In their position. In their situation. Think for a moment of the Golden Rule: treat others as we'd like to be treated. That's empathy.

If we're a stranger, would we welcome hospitality? Or a prisoner? Or a torture victim? Although we may not be able to share the feeling, we just think of what we would like to be done to us.

That's empathy. The motivation to prompt action to transcend our inertia. Caring for others, with action. Practicing hospitality, not just thinking of it. Isn't that the life of Jesus? When is the last time we expressed hospitality to strangers?

Frankly, my introverted personality likes to hide and remain private. But after reading this passage some time ago, I reached out to a stranger at church who was alone. We had a brief conversation, got separated, but ended up sitting across the aisle. I broke through my introversion, only to discover we had graduated from the same college. Not only that, one of the profs he had is a friend of mine. The connection felt good. I like to feel good. He seemed equally blessed.

It's been a long time since I visited anyone in prison. A long time. I do think of those who are mistreated and sometimes support ministries that work with them. But at an arm's distance.

Maybe I need to practice more hospitality.

Kick-Starting the Application

How natural is showing hospitality to you? What keeps you from doing more of it? What can encourage you to do more of it?

25—SEEK HELP

In my pride and independence and self-reliance, I sometimes resist asking for help. Okay, for decades, that was my default setting. But a needed lesson in humility hit me back in the mid-1980s. Sheila and I went to visit her mom in Spearville, Kansas, just east of Dodge City, but with a surprise. Oh, she knew we were coming, but to avoid her worrying we somehow forgot to mention we were riding our 1978 Honda Goldwing motorcycle. She saw us pull up out front, and joy and fear danced across her face.

She was shocked her daughter would attempt such a dangerous adventure. She knew her son-in-law rode but thought Sheila only did local rides. Yet before the trip ended, we convinced her to try it, so she climbed onto the passenger seat for a ride to see Sheila's brother, about 15 miles away. And back. She smiled a lot ... once she relaxed.

But as Sheila and I finally headed home on a Saturday, we hadn't gone far before the bike began to wobble some ... the back tire had a slow leak. I looked for a nail but couldn't find one, so I poured some water on the stem and found the small leak came from the inner tube. We slowly limped into the next small town, searching in vain for a properly sized replacement inner tube, but we did purchase a foot pump.

Few Kansas small towns have motorcycle shops, and not many auto part stores carry motorcycle tubes, so we faced a serious issue.

With most towns about twenty miles apart, we could travel twelve to fifteen miles before the tire deflated and we had to stop and pump it back up. Keeping the tire inflated was a lot of work in the Kansas heat, but repeating the pattern kept us moving.

We kept up that routine for 60 miles until we reached the panhandle of Oklahoma. I did some calling to nearby larger towns and found a small bike shop in Dalhart, Texas, about 30 miles away, that had the right tube. The shop promised to hold it and stay open until we arrived. They would be closed on Sunday, so we had to hurry.

The lady owner ran the front, and her husband did the wrenching, but he was gone on a Christian Motorcycle Association (CMA) ride for several more days. So, the shop had no trained mechanic to remove the rear wheel from the drive shaft and brakes and replace the tube. I'm a rider, not a wrencher. I had brought along the shop manual, but not many tools.

I gulped down a large helping of pride, acknowledged my ignorance, and almost begged if I could use the garage to do the dirty deed, in temps that passed 100. She smiled, said she knew less than me, the insurance company wouldn't like it, but she would allow it. She did seem to enjoy the show I put on. Sheila grabbed cold drinks from a nearby store, then passed me the tools.

We finally got the job done, and the bike got us home. Through this experience, I discovered desperation gives courage to us all. Even the courage to ask for aid. And upon getting home, I soon joined the CMA.

But beyond the repair, I learned to transcend my innate traits of independence and self-reliance. I grew up with pioneers from both sides of my family (one great-grandfather wrestled a grizzly—and won). My dad pulled his own teeth. A great-great-grandfather served frontier Kentucky as pastor ... and sheriff. Strength came with my DNA. Even today, we need godly independence, strength, and self-reliance to stand on our own two feet because we answer to God as individuals.

Honestly though, I often took those good traits too far, into hyper-individualism, avoiding the essential traits of having enough courage and humility to ask for help when needed. Three concepts changed my life.

First, know God cares deeply about the smallest details of our lives. Some of us who know him still often go it alone, thinking God's got enough work with a universe to run. That thinking minimizes both his love and omnipotent ability to multitask. Jesus's words convict me: "Are not two sparrows sold for a penny? Yet not one of them will fall to the ground outside your Father's care ... So don't be afraid; you are worth more than many sparrows" (Matthew 10:29,31).

Knowing God loves and cares destroys our lone-wolf inclination. The next step is our intentional connection with other followers so we can help and be helped with our innate and essential requirement for connection. First Corinthians 12:27 tell us, "Now you are *the body of Christ*, and *each one of you is a part* of it." Read that chapter to get the full impact of our interconnectedness with one another as the body of Jesus. I've yet to see a New Testament example of a lone-wolf follower of Jesus. God designed the Christian life to thrive with intimate connections with others.

Why? Because connections make us part of a body stronger than we are, and we rely on one another when in any kind of need. Acts 20:35 reads, "I showed you that by this kind of hard work *we must help the weak*." Who are the weak? Anyone in any kind of need. The lady in Dalhart helped this biker who was in dire need. She didn't know me and would never see me again this side of heaven, but in faith she helped.

Keep in mind, the flip side of giving help, discussed in the last chapter, is seeking it. Not to abuse it but to use it, to humbly seek help in genuine need. Sometimes, God provides the help through human hands that get blessed for it.

Kick-Starting the Application

How easily do you ask for help? What most keeps you from it? What role does pride play in it? If you struggle with pride, like I do, does it have a negative impact on the rest of your spiritual life? What most keeps you from letting God be God?

26—YOU GAVE US

Frankly, our natural world is being abused. Our biker group rode through the spine of California in June 2021, the magnificent Sierra Nevada Mountains. I cried. A lot. A natural and understandable reaction to seeing thousands of acres, sometimes stretching to the horizon, of beautiful forests burned in just the last year. Soon after our ride, two more major holocausts, the Dixie and Caldor fires, and numerous smaller ones continued the devastation.

Caldor, likely caused by a spark from a bullet strike on a rock, continued for two months, burned 221,835 acres, and destroyed one town.[1] Dixie, caused by a tree falling on a power line, was worse, burning 963,309 acres and destroying three communities.[2]

The year 2023 reached the hottest recorded annual temperature. Ever. Much of that we humans have caused. But is it just a climate change issue or a deeper spiritual one? My thoughts in this poem flowed out of my rides and observations of the state of our world.

> You gave us
>   a magnificent and intricate world
> rivers crystal clear for our thirst
>   and we dump waste in them

forests that cover our planet
> creating the oxygen we breathe
> and we burn them down through carelessness and greed

atmosphere that invigorates us with each breath
> and we foul it with our fumes

hills that curve like a woman's hips
> and we gouge into them to build more houses
> and see the earth erode into the sea

your breath breathed into ours
> into our spirits
> and we degrade our lives with
> excess ambition
> selfishness
> and we stupefy our lives with
>> intoxicants of all modes
>> addiction to entertainment that dulls our
> marvelous minds
> and we reject this gracious Giver

And I wonder
> would You sit back
> arms folded
> smile
> and say,
>> "It's still very good"?

We who ride experience the degradation more intimately. I smelled the charred trees as we stopped to view them. I saw the miles and miles of destroyed forest with each turn of the road. I stepped in ash on a roadside stop.

And frankly, the devastation goes further with more and stronger storms. As I write this, on January 9, 2024, I-70 in eastern Colorado and much of Kansas was closed for 450 miles. Multiple tornadoes devastated northern Florida, with 75 percent of their counties under a state of emergency.[3] One tornado impacted some of my family.

So, why might these natural disasters be a spiritual issue?

After each of the first five days creating, God sat back and said, "That's good." Another day of work brought humans into the scene, and again he sat back and raised the praise higher, saying, "That's very good."

Then he gave us a task: "The LORD God took the man and put him in the Garden of Eden *to work it and take care of it*" (Genesis 2:15). How have we done taking care of the world God provided to supply our needs? Not to despoil it, not to ruin it, but to take care of it for future generations?

God didn't yield ownership of the natural world—he just gave us the use of it, with accountability. The old term *stewardship* applies here, meaning we take care of another's property for the owner's interests. Stewardship is much like what we now call a "fiduciary responsibility," defined by Webster as "a relationship in which one party places special trust, confidence, and reliance in and is influenced by another who has a fiduciary duty to act for the benefit of the party."[4]

Let's explore the meaning of stewardship by examining Jesus's words:

> Who then is the faithful and wise manager [steward], whom the master puts in charge of his servants to give them their food allowance at the proper time? It will be good for that servant whom the master finds doing so when he returns ... But suppose the servant says to himself, "My master is taking a long time in coming," and he then begins to beat the other servants, both men and women, and to eat and drink and get drunk. The master of that servant will come on a day when he does not expect him and at an hour he is not aware of. He will cut him to pieces and assign him a place with the unbelievers. (Luke 12:42–43, 45–46)

We gain two key truths here. God gives us authority with what he provides. The steward oversaw the master's property, paid the bills, supervised the workers, and controlled the finances. But that authority comes with accountability, doesn't it? God will evaluate what we do with his resources, reward those who manage them well, and punish those who use them selfishly for their own benefit.

Let's get specific about what we steward. Clearly, taking care of the earth fits in, according to the earlier verse we examined, "The Lord God took the man and put him in the Garden of Eden to work it and take care of it" (Genesis 2:15). Too often, we increase our short-term profit and benefit by not taking the earth's health into account. Our population growth has caused many problems, but our technological growth allows us to identify the causes and resolve them.

But we are also stewards of the truth about God and his message of love to all people: "This, then, is how you ought to regard us: as servants [stewards] of Christ and as those entrusted with the mysteries God has revealed. Now it is required that those who have been given a trust must prove faithful" (1 Corinthians 4:1–2). Are we faithful and intentional in telling people what they don't know about God?

Honestly, too many of us have not understood that accepting Jesus as Lord, or boss, means we become stewards of what he has given, the earth and the good news. Those need to top our priority list. May he find us faithful.

KICK-STARTING THE APPLICATION

Do you see stewardship of the earth as a spiritual issue? Why or why not? Has this chapter influenced your thoughts? How committed have you been to creation care? What specific steps do you take now to care for the earth? In what ways might you do more to honor God by helping fellow humans take care of this world? And how are you doing as a steward of the message about Jesus? How intentional are you?

27—WHEN FEAR COST ME A BEER

In chapter three of my earlier book, *God, a Motorcycle, and the Open Road*, I told how I pulled into Groton, Connecticut, looking for a bar to view Nixon's resignation during Watergate. If you have the book, you can pull out that chapter to get the story in detail. But briefly, this long-haired hippie biker walked into a bar full of folks that looked like rednecks, realized that situation wasn't necessarily healthy for a hippie, and figured he better get out of Dodge. So, I quickly reversed my course and walked down the entry hallway, only to see a burly guy turn into the other end of the dark hallway.

I stepped to my left to give him room, and he also shifted, to remain right in front of me. I stepped to my right, then he did too. A direct look is often seen as a challenge, so I just glanced at him, raised my hands in peace, and said, "I don't mean anything by this." He did the same, raising his hands also.

That "burly guy" was my own reflection in a mirror, only looking burly from the large jacket for the chilly outside weather. I scared myself. Yeah, one tough biker!

Then in 2019, Sheila and I toured the Northeast, from Maine down to DC. A lot had changed. The two-lane road that I took into Groton had become I-95, but as we approached the town, I noticed the sign signifying the business route. Could that be the original highway?

"Sheila, let's try to find the Grotto. This may be the road." I had repeated the story earlier that day, so she agreed, and we exited. Bingo! That business I-95 was the same road from 1974, 45 years later. I slowed down, checking out each building. Then I found one that COULD have been the Grotto, but like I said, things change.

Fortunately, a mail carrier just happened to be working his route, so when he approached, I stepped up to him. "Sir, do you know if this building was the Grotto bar?"

Taken aback, he said, "The Grotto? Were you a local? It's not been called the Grotto for decades, but this isn't it. Go one block down. The same family still runs it. They now call it Christopher's."

Well, I found the Grotto, and we walked in. I noticed the hallway had been taken out and some other walls too. I then asked the waitress about the changes, and she said her father ran it then. She runs it now and had updated it to a restaurant bar. I then gulped and recounted my story from decades before to her.

She laughed and said, "You should have hung around. They weren't rednecks—they just didn't recognize you. They probably would have bought you a beer!" And honestly, her response made the story even better. Not only did I scare myself, but my fear cost me a free beer.

For 45 years, I thought the experience focused on fear, which was valid. I had real fear, even though the threat was only in my imagination. But this encounter taught me something new, which was the danger of first impressions and how they can cost us. First impressions may be lasting, but they can easily lead us astray. Me losing out on a free beer is pretty minor, but think of all we might lose by sticking to our false first impressions.

Truly, we need to be wise and not instantly trust people. Neither should we instantly mistrust them. Maybe instead we should probe below first impressions to learn the truth and how we can minimize the dangers of initial false evaluations.

First, let's be aware how our past experiences shape our perceptions. Two days before the first Grotto adventure, a cop in Utica, New York, stopped me for no reason, just to hassle a biker, saying he thought the bike might be stolen. "Conveniently," his system was down, so he wanted to arrest me and take me to the station. When we got there, the desk sergeant chewed him out and apologized, but I walked into the Grotto already a bit leery. We call that prejudice—some of my prejudging of the Grotto came from my recent experience with the cop.

So, how do we deal with initial interpretations? When we feel tempted to judge the first impression, slow down and learn more. I walked out too soon and shouldn't have ... and only learned the facts 45 years later. God tells us not to judge too quickly: "In a lawsuit the first to speak seems right, until someone comes forward and cross-examines" (Proverbs 18:17).

The principle means we take some time when we can to see the entirety of the situation. I gave them one look only and lost a beer.

Also, give some grace. Let your default be to give people a chance—unless we find huge warning signs. God doesn't call us to be stupid. But I never gave the guys in the bar a chance to buy me a beer, even to harass me, because I assumed they had bad motives. I was wrong and lost out.

A earlier politician encouraged us to trust, but verify. Our temptation is to look first at what we see. But maybe we should act like God: "But the Lord said to Samuel ... 'People look at the outward appearance, but the Lord looks at the heart'" (1 Samuel 16:7). Let's give people a chance beyond our first impressions, take some time, and get to know the real situation.

Do we desire to know the truth? Finding out the truth can take some work.

If you read my first book, you now know "the rest of the story."

KICK-STARTING THE APPLICATION

Think of a time when you judged a person or situation too quickly, to your detriment. What influenced your quick judgment? How could you have handled the situation with more wisdom? Is it too late to go back to some of these and make them right? How can you probe beneath the first and surface impression?

28—A SNOWY PASS

By Toby Erickson, retired schoolteacher, author, biker

My path home took me from Oroville in Northern California to Spokane, Washington. The route included beautiful mountains and scenery through central Oregon toward Bend. The "iffy" April weather could bring some rain or some sunshine, but I hoped for no snow.

Riding through a snowstorm on a motorcycle doesn't qualify as advisable, particularly a Gold Wing GL1800 loaded with gear. I'm not sure if my anxiety exacerbated my cold skin under my layers of protective gear, but I was shivering.

The snow started lightly as I left the busy I-5 at Weed, California, and started east on the lonely Highway 97, heading toward the windy pass between Klamath Falls and Bend. The lack of traffic made me question my decision to ride on as I wondered, "Why am I the only one out here?" My prayers for protection, guidance, and traction continued in earnest.

Then the snow began to build with larger and larger flakes falling on me, the bike, and the road. Some accumulation seemed to be occurring on my windscreen and the shoulder of the road. The road itself, however, just looked wet. Moving slowly, I was watching for places to ditch the bike should I start to lose traction. Unsure of what lay ahead, I determined to continue until I had better options to stop someplace warm. Then came the flashing highway sign: Chains Required Ahead.

A truck stop with a covered gas pump area and a convenience store came into view, so I decided this was a perfect place to reassess my situation. After parking the bike under some cover, I attempted to wipe the snow from my windscreen. It was completely iced over. Walking into the convenience store, I began thinking, "I'll bet I'm going to be living here for a while! My bike ain't going nowhere!"

I also expected the local folks to look at me in my snowed-over motorcycle and garb to say, "What kind of idiot rides a motorcycle in weather like this?"

A couple of ladies were working the store. One offered and then poured an encouraging hot cup of coffee as soon as I entered. The other gal looked up from stocking corn chips long enough to say, "Hey! Nice day for a ride?"

I asked Coffee Lady if she had any idea how long the storm and chain control might be in effect. She said, "Oh, this is nothing! Highway 97 won't require chains ... almost never does. Look here!"

She pulled out her phone and flipped through a few screens to show me an image from a live highway camera.

"The temp here is 39 degrees, so black ice isn't a problem. That's Crescent, just 20 miles down the hill. See, no snow! And La Pine, maybe another 20 minutes farther ... sunshine and 50 degrees. You're through the worst of it, buddy!"

Relief washed over me. I was through the worst, just when I thought I'd hit the worst. While doubt, fear, and anxiety were trying to ruin my day, God was carrying me through with the encouragement of these ladies—exactly what I needed.

Toby's story gives us a lot of spiritual links, and this passage helped him on this adventure—both during and reflecting on it later:

> Praise be to the God and Father of our Lord Jesus Christ, the Father of compassion and the God of all comfort, *who comforts us in all our troubles*, so that *we can comfort those in any trouble* with the comfort we ourselves receive from God. For just as we share abundantly in the sufferings of Christ, so also our comfort abounds through Christ. If we are distressed, it is for your comfort and salvation; if we are comforted, it is for your comfort, which *produces in you patient endurance* of the same sufferings we suffer" (2 Corinthians 1:3-6).

Some tips from Toby's experiences. First, expect troubles. They abound in life, and we riders know riding adds inherent dangers—mechanical issues, weather, hassles from others, risky riding, and more. There's no need to be surprised or frustrated by them. After all, we bikers fit into two categories—those who have gone down and those who are going down.

Second, trust in God to bring comfort, as the above passage says. No, he doesn't always end the difficulty, but he is with us and sees us through it. To my mind, his presence sometimes softens the trouble, and a sense of his presence can get us through a lot.

Third, realize he works in all trouble. Romans 8:28 reads, "And we know that in all things God works for the good of those who love him, who have been called according to his purpose." I've found he often uses people like the

Coffee Lady, circumstances, events, animals, or weather to communicate his presence and comfort to us.

Fourth, we can use the comfort he brings to build that patient endurance mentioned in verse six. Once we've worked our way through the hard times with his comfort, we gain confidence he will work for good in the next trouble. Granted, sometimes we'll never see the good in this lifetime, but I appreciate I can fit into his overall plan even when I don't understand it.

So, do you wonder how the rest of Toby's ride went? Well, he survived to write this, but here's the rest of the story, again in his words. "The weather looked to be much the same for the next day. I decided to have a sort of praise and worship service in the privacy of my helmet during that second long day of riding. When the weather was clear, I praised God for the sheer pleasure of riding in the sunshine. When the clouds darkened, and a bit of rain fell, I praised him all the same." Sounds like patient endurance to me.

KICK-STARTING THE APPLICATION

How do you typically respond when trouble comes? How has your response worked for you? Think of a trial when you saw God work. What effect did it have on your faith?

Toby Erickson resides with his wife near their grandchildren in eastern Washington. When not riding, he makes regular moto-camping tours to stay connected with his California family and enjoys woodworking, teaching Sunday school, and writing. He has also written *Raise Your Own Dang Kids!*

29—OUTDO ONE ANOTHER

John and his Harley D met me and my Goldwing at the 76 gas station in Temecula. Our destination? Head west to the mountains and down to the coast. Ironically, winter gives the best riding in SoCal. The temp doesn't get too high and stays mild. Usually. Winter rains turn the golden hills of California (some call it dead grass) into lush and green wild grasses. Our route: take Rancho California Road as it enters the mountains and join De Luz Road where the creek crosses seven times. Well, the creek crossings happen in wet years. This year gave us enough rain to bring the green, but not much water.

Curves and oaks and horse ranches and hills slowed us down enough to enjoy the view, and the bikes kept us moving at a good pace where we could enjoy the marriage of road, rider, and bike. John and I may have left the ages of high testosterone and sport bikes, but no one passed us.

About 10 miles in, the trees opened up on a straight long enough to reveal a quick glimpse of what looked to be another bike, only to quickly hide it. Instinctively, I cranked the throttle to catch him. I still love speed and competition, but our previous pace let us enjoy the route, and I backed off. Some. More glimpses let me know we slowly closed the gap, and I smiled.

As we approached an intersection, the trees opened up again, and I saw only 50 yards separated us. I smiled again, glad we still gained on him, but this time, he noticed us. The trees and curves blocked our view for a while, then I clearly saw down the road maybe 100 yards. No biker in sight, no place to turn off. He saw the "competition" getting closer, and he sped up noticeably.

I felt proud I fought off the temptation to race, proud that at our normal pace we gained on him. He likely felt proud two old guys didn't pass him. We both won this unspoken competition.

In bitter lessons, oft-repeated, I've discovered competition can both tempt and test me. In my earlier years, winning competitions seemed to support my frail ego, which caused unhealthy and selfish relationships—temptations. Friendships got damaged by it, and winning the competitions did nothing to solve the low self-confidence.

But I still like the chance to challenge myself, to push my limits, to stretch them—tests. Methods to assess how I'm doing versus only myself. My Iron Butt ride at 70 was a personal test. Temptations are unhealthy. Tests can be good. But what does God say about competition?

Loving competition and following Jesus, I figured I should discover that. Does God call competition good or negative? Let's look at a passage that addresses interpersonal competition.

"Each one should test their own actions. Then they can take pride in themselves alone, *without comparing themselves* to someone else" (Galatians 6:4). This verse destroyed my entire process of gaining pride from competing against others. Pride coming from seeing how we stack up next to others is counterfeit and ungodly.

We can make a distinction for competitions like judging who may be the GOAT, the greatest of all time, in athletics or determining which job candidate has the best qualifications. Those are valid, as long as they're not the basis of our pride and worth. Paul, in the 1 Corinthians passage, said pride was problematic when we compare ourselves to others.

But let's flip the script to see the other side of the story—God does value competition! Honestly, this surprised me, God encourages us to compete with others. Ready for a surprise? His view on competition may not be what you think.

Very simply, Paul tells us to "honor one another above yourselves" (Romans 12:10). Other translations more openly suggest an outright competition in showing each other honor. Hmmm. Compete with one another. Not by showing you're better, but by seeing who can best value and respect the other. Gosh, we need this today, don't we, in our age of road rage, division, crime, and more.

What does it mean to show honor? Let's look at the context, Romans 12:10–20, of the commands Paul gave defining the showing of honor. I'm not providing any commentary, just God's words on how to compete. And as you read each, test your actions. Ask the Holy Spirit to give you some nudges. How well do you do in each? Which ones most cry out for improvement?

Verse 10: "Be devoted to one another in love."

Verse 13: "Share with the Lord's people who are in need."

Verse 13: "Practice hospitality."

Verse 14: "Bless those who persecute you."

Verse 15: "Rejoice with those who rejoice; Mourn with those who mourn."

Verse 16: "Live in harmony with one another."

Verse 16: "Be willing to associate with people of low position."

Verse 16: "Do not be conceited."

Verse 17: "Do not repay anyone evil for evil."

Verse 18: "As far as it depends on you, live at peace with everyone."

So, for all of you who love competing, here are two tips. First, compete against yourself. Check out your attitudes and test your actions to find your limits and needed growth areas. Take pride when you give honor in these behaviors. Second, compete in blessing others. On the road, maybe let that guy in. At the market, smile at the checker when she makes a mistake. Be a godly winner. And maybe we can make showing honor contagious. Now that is a fine competition.

KICK-STARTING THE APPLICATION

How competitive are you? What general areas do you most and least compete in? Does competition increase your pride and self-worth? Why? Have you ever considered competition to be godly? Of the list of commands associated with competing to show honor, which can you take godly pride in? Which do you most need to work on? What practical steps can you take to work on them this week?

30—A DAY IN THE LIFE OF BIKERS

This chapter will feature no great event, like being pulled over by cops with drawn guns as told in the previous book, *God, a Motorcycle, and the Open Road*. No heart-stopping fear like in that same book when this hippie biker strolled into a redneck bar (but chapter 27 does have a surprising resolution 45 years after it happened). Yet it has something likely better—an example of how to discover God touches in everyday life.

Several years ago, our church's biker group scheduled a putt after our men's breakfast, heading from Temecula west to the coast and then south and back, about 100 miles. Steve, our pastor, came to see us off and hopped on a bike for a photo op. An auspicious pastoral send-off for what we hoped would be a fine ride.

We pulled out of town with a warm temp of 95, on De Luz Road through the mountains to Fallbrook, then down North River Road through delightful flower fields, nurseries, and dairies to Oceanside. The powers that be had realigned some streets, so once we had to backtrack a little, but we safely arrived at the coast. Traffic wasn't too bad on the 20 miles or so south to Del Mar, and we took several stops to view the ocean. Del Mar was our turnaround point, and then we went east through Rancho Santa Fe and skirted Dixon Lake where we grabbed lunch at a one-time favorite Mexican restaurant before heading north on the historic Highway 395 back home.

The God touches? Our first shady road wove through a stream seven times, under the canopy of sycamores and oaks, then we crested a hill with marvelous views of colorful flower and crop fields. The scent of salty ocean water cleared our sinuses, and we passed ranches with horses romping. God's gift of a beautiful world touched us. We appreciated the order in a universe that could produce motorcycles to best enjoy it. And our coastal route was a good 20 degrees nicer than the temp of 95 back in Temecula.

I call that worship—seeing and appreciating God's touch. Good stuff. Lunch didn't match that. Two of us had been to the restaurant before and were eager to return. Maybe we offended our server by asking for separate checks, because from there the meal went downhill. The food took at least half an hour to arrive—and then all at different times. Ruben, the last to be served, finally bit into his beef taco, only to discover some sneaky white meat. Chicken. Ten more minutes for that to get replaced. Some of us finished eating before Ruben even received his proper order.

And yes, we kept our attitudes positive and left tips well above normal. A chance for another God touch. Do we respond with his grace or our frustration? Thankfully, we chose the former, but none of us are likely to return.

The lesson of the day? Life blends ups and downs. A marvelous world. Hot temperatures. A surly and slow server. Do we choose to let the garbage bog us down and steal our joy, or do we do our best and move along? But how do we accomplish making the best of bad things?

First, know that a lot of bad exists in the world, and our slow and surly server merely serves as a metaphor for much worse events. Wars. School shootings. Political partisanship. Road rage. Sometimes good can turn into bad on the turn of a dime. Life is like a pigeon—we never know when crap might drop on us. Sometimes we happen to be in the wrong place at the wrong time. Sometimes it's from a deliberate choice on our or others' parts.

Expect those struggles. First Peter 4:12 tells us, "Dear friends, *do not be surprised at the fiery ordeal that has come on you to test you*, as though something strange were happening to you." When we expect only good to occur, disappointment can take away the joy of God's presence.

Second, know a lot of good exists as well. The ride had some great times, and like the bad, life is a pigeon that sometimes drops good stuff. See Matthew 5:45: "He causes his sun to rise on the evil and the good, and sends rain on the righteous and the unrighteous." Good comes to all.

Perhaps the key comes from looking for the good. Cherish the sunshine, the rain, the mountains and valleys, the sunsets and sunrises. Let them all quietly shout where they came from. This book and my blog, *Unconventional*, at timriter.com, are encouragements to see small God touches in daily life, to become aware of how he blesses us even as Satan tries to tear us apart.

Third, know we can choose peace amid difficulties. We can make that choice by recognizing the reality of both good and bad, yet focusing our thoughts on the positive: "Finally, brothers and sisters, whatever is true, whatever is noble, whatever is right, whatever is pure, whatever is lovely, whatever is admirable—if anything is excellent or praiseworthy—*think about such things* ... And *the God of peace will be with you*" (Philippians 4:8–9).

What result comes when we choose to focus on the positive while acknowledging the reality of pain? God and his peace will dominate our thoughts and emotions. Emotions typically flow from how we interpret events, so we can maintain our joy in hard times when we interpret evil as part of life, a life where in the end God wins.

So, look for the God touches that bless you. And look for the chances for you to be the touch of God in the life of someone who needs it.

KICK-STARTING THE APPLICATION

Think of a recent time that started good and went south. Which lasted the longest in your memory? What might that reveal about yourself? How often do you seek out God touches or even look for them? For chances to be a God touch? You might want to memorize Philippians 4:8–9 that we mentioned above.

31—FOLLOW YOUR LEADERS?

For a year or so, several guys who ride from our church joined in on rides with a biker group from another church. We made up quite a motley crew with a variety of bikes, mostly Harleys and Hondas with some others. Some had touring bikes, some sport bikes, and some adventure ones. Even a dirt bike on occasion. Our group also came with a nice range of ages, and while I may have been the old guy, some hadn't escaped their 20s. The two churches differed on several issues of style and structure, but both agreed on the essentials.

Most importantly, we bonded over a shared a love of bikes and Jesus. We enjoyed stopping at overlooks or meals, had great fellowship, and made new friendships. We were one group, not two separate groups riding together, a nice metaphor of the unity Jesus wants from all his followers, as it says in John 13:35: "By this everyone will know that you are my disciples, if you love one another." This concept complements the chapter "Two-Wheeled Unity" from the first book, but we're now taking this story in a different direction.

Then an accident on one ride added an important spiritual lesson to the great companionship. We left Temecula heading southeast for the scenic town of Ramona. (Names have been changed to protect the guilty.)

Howard, our leader, picked out a route ahead of time, one he'd not yet ridden, entered it on his GPS, and off we went, four Harleys and three Hondas on this putt. In the hills south of Temecula, leaving the small community of Rainbow, he approached an intersection and went straight. One followed, while the other five of us, wondering why he'd done that, stopped and pulled over to the side to wait.

Why? Well, most of us had been on that road, and we ALL saw the No Outlet sign on the straight route. After waiting probably five minutes, we sent a rider to find our lost leader, and Howard soon joined us with a sheepish grin, saying, "My GPS was slow in telling me to turn left." Well, he's a football coach, so we let missing the sign slide ... not. After all, we are bikers. Not a lot of mercy at times.

Sadly, that mistake came with a cost. The dead end led to a narrow road, and when the wayward riders did their U-turn, the follower, Kent, dropped his bike, a pretty heavy one. It landed on his leg and caused a bruise that hurt too much to continue the ride, so he headed back the five miles on his own.

His wife saw the bruise and convinced him to get it examined. The doctors found a small break in a bone. That was his last ride, but honestly, don't blame the leader, as getting injured could have happened any time or place. But missing the sign provides our lesson on leaders who might lead us astray.

In life, our leaders will make mistakes, will take us on dead ends or the wrong route. Two examples of many include the failure of the Willow Creek Church leadership to deal with sexual morality issues and the leadership of the Roman Catholic Church concealing claims of sexual abuse. In both cases, the consequences touched and damaged many people.

Other mistakes don't qualify as that crucial. For instance, maybe starting a program that didn't meet the needs of people or wasn't administered properly or one that stayed too long after its effectiveness had disappeared. So, how do we follow flawed leaders? Remember, all leaders possess flaws—in differing degrees. Let's explore three suggestions.

First, respect their leadership roles and the gifts that brought them to their positions. This doesn't require blind obedience—most of us stopped when Howard made the wrong turn. But our attitude should be supportive. See Hebrews 13:17 (MSG): "Be responsive to your pastoral leaders. Listen to their counsel. They are alert to the condition of your lives and work under the strict supervision of God. Contribute to the joy of their leadership, not its drudgery."

After spending decades pastoring, I found some members made serving a joy. Some others made it a drudgery. Maybe our default approach to leaders should be supporting them in prayer and service rather than looking for their problems.

Second, evaluate how serious the mistake is. For minor ones, like missing a turn, and for most methods and matters of opinion, we can usually just go along for the sake of unity. First Peter 4:8 says, "Above all, love each other deeply, because *love covers over a multitude of sins.*" Maybe instead of critiquing them, we should pray for and encourage our leaders.

But serious mistakes, like with Willow Creek and the abuse in the Catholic church, call us to confront them. Don't just leave—seek to restore: "Brothers and sisters, if someone is caught in a sin, you who live by the Spirit should restore that person gently" (Galatians 6:1). That "someone" includes leaders, doesn't it?

And notice the goal—restoration. That means we work for confession and repentance, not immediate firing or leaving the church. When restoration occurs, we move on together. Realize healing can take time, so be as patient with them as God is with us. But if that restoration doesn't come, then follow the directions of your GPS: "Recalculating." But as the final option, not the first.

Third, a word to leaders. If your followers don't follow, examine your own actions and determine why they don't follow your leadership. Find out the why. Spend time in prayer. Speak to mature believers who know the situation. The problem may be your followers, or it may be you.

Leaders have a vital importance in the church, but we don't blindly follow. Why? We stand as individuals at the judgment seat of God.

KICK-STARTING THE APPLICATION

Think of a time a church leader took a wrong turn, either personally or with the church. What was your response—did you ignore it, overreact, or handle it well? Was it a mistake that could be overlooked or a more serious one? Did grace and truth combine? How could you have dealt with the situation more effectively?

32—OUR VAST AND VARIED WORLD

Pulling out of Temecula onto I-15 at 4 a.m. back in 2018, I had one primary goal. To test myself, to push my limits, to see if at 70 I could repeat the feat I'd done at 28: riding over 1,000 miles on two wheels in under 24 hours. Oh yeah, I had other goals, like to meet Jerry in Butte as we headed east to bag three states I had not yet ridden in, and then to meet Mick and Brad and head to Banff. Honestly, this primary goal topped the list as a personal issue—me against the road and my age. But the trip also brought an unexpected result.

Dawn had not yet broken before I completed the first segment to Barstow, but the darkness held no issues for me. With little traffic heading to St. George, I had the leisure to notice the desert beauty in the pre-dawn—subtle shades of differing colors on the mountains and hills. Varying hues of green vegetation. The uniquely eroded rock shapes. The vivid three-dimensionality only the arid deserts give. Then came the stunner—the morning sun striking the red rock cliffs around St. George. I had to stop for a quick pic.

The cliffs yielded to the wide farming valleys farther north, with lush alfalfa and grazing cattle and horses. The bigger cities, Provo and Salt Lake, offered neither much scenery nor punishment, merely a small drizzle in Provo, but the Wasatch mountains to the east provided a nice touch of majesty. The pass north of Salt Lake took me to yet another higher and different area. Ranches and cattle in Idaho, then Montana and its rolling hills and valleys and mountains captivated me, as always. Trees covered the hills, the sunset over the Rockies to the west took my breath, and I felt at home. After over 16 hours on the bike, I smiled at the sight of the Motel 6, my home for a night.

Yes, I met the test: 1,080 miles. But then serendipity struck. Seeing all that country over two or three days would have segmented it, but doing it all in one day transformed it into a unity. Temecula, California, to Dillon, Montana. A whole, in one day. The vastly differing geographies, climates, times of day, all flowed into a whole. And perceiving it in its wholeness changed my perception. The variety struck me. And deeper yet, viewing this holistically taught me something about God. So here are, for the first time, my Iron Butt lessons about the person of God.

First, God loves beauty. The beauty of the created world continues to amaze me, and he created us to appreciate that beauty. May we not forget that with God, beauty takes a multitude of forms. The deserts with their dimensions and colors and shapes and arid air make everything crisp. The valleys produce growing crops, give rivers their course, and provide homes. The mountains gift us with water, and their trees gift us with oxygen and point us to God. The glory of sunrises and sunsets. And, most importantly, the variety of people, in all our forms and ways of laughing and living.

We all have our favorite sources of beauty. I understand that. But maybe we can extend our range and begin to appreciate more. I promise you, as you stretch your envelope of what beauty you appreciate, you'll gain a much deeper understanding of God. Look for all the beauty God gives and blesses us with. Then, take it deeper: What does his love of beauty tell you about him, his transcendence, his love, his character, his provision?

Second, I saw the world as a unity—to a greater degree than I normally do on any trip. Yes, we see the world as one in theory when we see a globe or map. We get the big picture, but those merely represent the world. In one day, traveling nearly 1,100 miles, I experienced its vastness in a way I never had before. I saw and smelled and touched and heard and covered a LOT of his world. That changed me. Yet even that huge run composes less than 5 percent of the earth's circle. However, all aspects connect to each other.

The same principle can extend to the entire earth. Yeah, I can't do that in one day on a motorcycle. Yet a recent flight with a window seat from San Diego to Anchorage, Alaska, over 2,400 miles all in daylight, from sunrise to sunset, gave me a similar God's-eye view, seeing a lot of creation in one day. And the more we travel, the more we're able to see more of God's majesty.

What a magnificent God to create such a united world, so different, but balanced. The cycle of water—remaining basically the same total, but evaporating from the surface liquid into cloud vapor, then falling as rain and snow and hail to replenish the lakes and streams and rivers and underground water table. The same water is in each step, just in varying forms and locations. Then we have the food chain, beginning with plants adapting energy from the sun and turning it into plant energy to feed grass-eating animals who then feed meat-eating animals who then die and fertilize the plants.

So, here's the takeaway. Do I suggest you all buy a motorcycle and do an Iron Butt ride? Of course not. But look at the world. Really look. Look for what it says about the One who made it. Maybe take some long trips and see each day, not as a unit, but just one phase of the united overall journey. Look for God's footprints.

KICK-STARTING THE APPLICATION

From this chapter, what did you learn about God and the world? What intrigued you about the concept of a vast and varied and united world? Have you experienced a similar epiphany of seeing God in the natural world he created? How can you learn more? And as you travel, can you intentionally look for what nature reveals about God?

33—FIGHTING FEAR PAYS OFF

By Deb Terasaki, biker, Bible study leader

I have always been afraid of riding on a motorcycle. When I was a teenager, a friend's dad took me for a ride. "Just hang on and lean" was his command. He swerved left and right, expecting me to lean into the turns, but I feared falling off. Later I met Don, who became my husband. Don had a bike and rode with friends from the Harley group. Riding was important to Don, so I rode too. Still terrified, I tried to swallow my fear but remained concerned about falling off. Once he bought a trike, I grew much more comfortable about riding. With no more sitting completely still and leaning, I felt so much safer now.

My husband Don has been riding over 40 years, and since retiring, he rides out every morning to meet his fellow bikers. Soon after he departed one day, my phone rang with a call from him. How odd, normally he would text me but not call ... he should be riding to the Harley shop to meet with his fellow riders. I answered the phone, but no one was on the other end. I began to text him to figure this out, and again my phone rang. It was my husband, but no one answered on the other end. I got worried and tried to call, but then the phone rang again with Don's voice. "I wrecked my bike," he said.

"Are you okay?"

"No, but the ambulance is coming."

Immediately, I prayed for the angels to protect him and guide my decisions and actions. Friends were called to head to the accident until I could arrive. As soon as I got there, the ambulance rushed him to the hospital. The guardian angels had worked overtime. The left lane of traffic had backed up, but a driver thought he could zip across the three lanes of traffic and never expected to see a motorcycle coming toward him. But suddenly, he saw Don coming in the right-hand lane as his car approached that lane of traffic. Too late to stop, Don swerved right and hit the curb.

His bike flipped twice and landed on its side against a tree. He flipped twice in the other direction and landed on his bottom ... in his first accident. It is truly a miracle he did not suffer more injuries. He had broken all the ribs on the left side and had a bad scrape on his forearm, but otherwise he was okay.

The outpouring of prayers for healing and help guided us as we dealt with all the accident entailed. Angels protected Don in what could have been much more severe and life-threatening. Don is not yet a believer, but I know God's hand was there.

Don? He is planning on more long trips. I don't think he is healed enough to ride, but he is a stubborn guy. Like most bikers, he'll face down his fears and won't give in. Hmmm, I guess I've faced down my fears too.

Fear plays a key role in life. We all have some, but some have more. Fears seem to change depending on our life stages and experiences. *Simply Psychology* helps explain fear, calling it "a basic, emotional response to a perceived threat or danger ... Fear is an essential survival mechanism, helping individuals react to potentially life-threatening situations."[1]

Fear, real or imagined, can bring physical effects. Even thinking we're in danger of losing something, our dignity, our life, our finances, or anything else, is enough. Frankly, all of us who ride face increased danger. That's reality—just ask Don and Deb. So, how do we face down our fears? Some tips, both for riding and life.

First, let fear be your friend. Use it as motivation to minimize the risks that needlessly increase the danger. Take the safety courses. Don't ride beyond your skill level. Take care of your tires and mechanicals. Grow in your riding ability. Like the *Simply Psychology* quote pointed out, fear can protect us from legitimate threats.

Second, avoid imagining threats about the future. For years, I'd play an unhealthy mental game called "What if this happens?" I grew fears from anticipating what might happen, most of which never did. Jesus addressed anticipating fears: "Therefore *do not worry about tomorrow*, for tomorrow will worry about itself. Each day has enough trouble of its own" (Matthew 6:34). Here's a caveat: we can wisely respond to fears about the future by doing what we can now to lessen what we fear.

Third, face them down, like Don and Deb did. Acknowledge their existence, take the precautions you can, and keep on keeping on. Fear can make us wise, but we don't have to allow it to disable us. When we have an important task or mission, we carry on. We acknowledge the fear, evaluate it, then continue with God's help.

That's the fourth tip—we gain strength to face all fears through God's presence:

> So do not fear, for I am with you;
> > do not be dismayed, for I am your God.
> I will strengthen you and help you.
> Isaiah 41:10)

God won't stop all the bad consequences, but from my experience, he often softens them. And always, he is with us, giving us the comfort of his presence and the power of his Spirit.

And fifth, live out the best expression of fear, "The *fear* of the Lord is the *beginning of wisdom*" (Psalm 111:10). The fear of the Lord, an awareness of his transcendence and feeling somewhat intimidated by his otherness, puts us in the center of a transformed life. I found 23 passages that use fearing God, biblically, as an antithesis, or opposite, to behaviors that displease him. Look up these four on your own: Leviticus 19:14, 25:17, 25:36, 25:43.

A part of life, fear can be our friend and our greatest connection to God.

Kick-Starting the Application

What are your largest fears? What makes them fearsome? What has worked for you in conquering fear? How can you better involve God in the process?

Deb Terasaki has been blessed to be involved in Bible studies through the years and, for the past five, has led one. Deb and her husband, Don, ride with fellow bikers in the Dallas Harley chapter. During their 40 years of marriage, they have shared the love of riding with many lifelong friends.

34—HOW EASY GOT HIS GROOVE BACK

I've enjoyed every bike I've owned, but my Honda ST1300 topped the list—a sport touring bike that was nimble around town and great on long rides. Carving mountain curves on it always caused a smile. The vehicle for my 2018 Iron Butt ride, my average speed, including stops, was 66 mph. Yes, the statute of limitations has passed, and that bike handled well over 100 mph as smoothly as 65. But the time came to put this steed out to pasture.

Fast cornering has long attracted me, that marvelous melding of man, machine, and road that brings such joy. Not to the point of stupidity though. I've never gone down at a speed above five mph. But then came Scott, a good friend and part of our church riding group. He knew mountain roads well, loved speed, and on the group rides on the twisties, he led with me on his tail and the rest of the group well behind us.

But upon entering my 70s, I realized keeping up with Scott concerned me. Decreasing balance and coordination stole my confidence in the corners, and I knew I couldn't slow down on that bike. The temptation to corner like I used to do safely would be a dragon rearing its head. Realizing a less aggressive bike might keep me upright and alive led me to the Honda Goldwing, with unsurpassed comfort and protection from rain, cold, and heat. A great bike—except on slow turns.

The loaded weight of 1,100 pounds caused me to drop it twice on city streets while moving under five mph, a new experience in my over 50 years of riding. But on my first long ride with it, heading east outside of Cambria, California, on a back road, I felt terror for the first time on a bike. The uphill and narrow road featured very sharp turns with a lot of potholes, some traffic, and headed into a sometimes-blinding sun. I didn't trust the bike or myself and several times had to stop and let it roll downhill to make a turn. Another back road east of Fort Ross matched that, and I was ready to sell the bike.

Then Jerry, my trusted riding companion and friend since high school, took me aside, and hesitantly and almost apologetically (remember, he's known me a long time) offered an observation. "Tim, I'm watching you from behind, and you're fighting the bike, you're leaning against it. Try leaning your body more into the turn with the bike."

Basic biker strategy, given to a guy who loved fast cornering. And had once been good at it, but no longer. So, I did some experimenting on the gentle curves of that section. Better.

At Yuba City, he went north and I east, heading for Highway 49 to Truckee. The road had some sharp curves, so I did more experimenting. Some said 15 mph, and they were ... fun. Again! Why? Easy Riter got his groove back—by listening.

The key life principle here? Listening to good advice improves our riding ... and our lives. But why?

Listening is a shortcut to avoid learning everything by ourselves. We choose to stand on the shoulders of those who have gone before. We use their lessons, tweak them to match our personalities, gifts, and life situations, and learn faster. Here's what God tells us to do:

Seek advice.

> Plans are established by *seeking advice*;
>   so if you wage war, obtain guidance.
> (Proverbs 20:18)

When we look to what comes next, first get the input of others. My future riding improved due to Jerry's advice. But Solomon told us not only to just listen to advice but also to seek it. We should take the initiative sometimes and have an openness when given it. But we also need to ...

Evaluate the advice. Not all counsel, offered or sought, is good. Think of Job's friends who advised him inaccurately about why he suffered. Evaluate the credibility of the advisors. Do they know their stuff on the subject? Jerry did, as a long-time rider. Also, examine their values. Do they match yours? They may still give good advice, but rival world values can hurt, as Proverbs warns us:

> The plans of the righteous are just,
>   but the advice of the wicked is deceitful.
> (Proverbs 12:5)

Sometimes advice is strengthened with other viewpoints:

> Plans fail for lack of counsel,
>   but with *many advisers* they succeed.
> (Proverbs 15:22)

Take the time to get the take of others.

Also, gauge yourself. Does the other know more than you? Do they offer a perspective you don't have? In my life, often I've been too proud and independent to either seek or listen to advice. Refusing advice has damaged me often, but I'm learning. It's a tough lesson at times, so be wiser than me.

> The way of fools seems right to them,
>   but the wise listen to advice.
> (Proverbs 12:15)

God also desired that when we get good advice, we ...

Do it. Don't just respond, "Yes, you're right," and then do what you want.

> Turn from evil and *do good*;
> seek peace and pursue it (Psalm 34:14).

Jerry had the courage to speak, and I listened because "wounds from a friend can be trusted" (Proverbs 27:6). Listening to good advice improved my riding ... and my life.

Yeah, this principle has some caveats. Trust the friend. Trust their insights. Trust they speak in love. Pray about it, and maybe get more input.

But it is *so* nice to have my groove back on a bike. Thanks, Jerry!

Kick-Starting the Application

How easy is it for you to listen to advice? Why? Might you have some issues with pride, as I do? Do you have some friends close enough to wound you in love? Think about the times a friend cautioned you, you listened, and their advice worked. What made the scenario turn out well? If it didn't work out, what caused that?

35—CREATION CARE

Life often changes quickly, moving from the best to the worst. Our Gray Hogs ride of June 2021 typified that. First the best stuff. We covered a lot of California's awe-inspiring Sierra Nevada mountains. On a side trip that Jerry and Nick chose to skip, the General Sherman tree, the largest single-stem tree on earth, and Sequoia National Park astounded Brad and me with their grandeur. Their loss. Lunch at the Sierra Nevada Brewery in Chico with the best fish and chips we'd ever had—so good two of us returned two years later. Yes, that good.

Also, we visited an exotic car rally in Auburn, featuring Lamborghinis, Ferraris, Porsches, a classic Ford Cobra, the new 'vettes, and more. Jerry and I were in heaven wandering among them, and we had a fine conversation with a Lambo owner. We traveled Tioga Pass through Yosemite to Lee Vining and Bridgeport with a lot of stops to look in wonder and traversed Sonora Pass, the Sierra pass that most impresses me, just above it.

A mechanic at a bike shop who replaced my worn rear tire provided some tips on tire inflation to help my ponderous Goldwing and Jerry's three-wheeled Can Am handle tight turns better. Mick and I visited California pioneer Peter

Lassen's grave. The Gray Hogs had great times laughing, teasing ... and eating.

The worst of times also showed up. Brad collided with a car in Auburn. Fortunately, he only experienced aches and pains without injuries, but his Goldwing got totaled, causing him to decide he'd reached the end his riding days. At the age of 82, Mick determined, for the second and final time, he'd reached his riding end, decreasing the Hogs core four to just Jerry and me. We share a lot of memories and stories, some in this book along with others in the earlier biker devo.

But the worst of the worst arrived with seeing miles of forest incinerated by the previous year's fires. In some places, burned pines and cedars covered all the ridges in sight.

This evidence showed us all isn't well on Planet Earth, but more of the worst was yet to come.

Riding south on 395, Lone Pine Creek was a small trickle, maybe one-fifth of its normal flow. Traffic jams slowed down Mick and me on both 395 and I-5. We're seeing more frequent and stronger storms, while other parts of our country face long droughts.

With the first five stages of creation, God pronounced them "good." Then with the creation of man in stage six, he proclaimed this was "very good." He gave us the earth to meet our needs and told us to take care of it in Genesis 2:15. I wonder—why would the very good damage the good? Let me share three foundational truths.

First, the climate is changing. We may disagree over what role mankind has played, but overwhelming evidence shows the reality of the change. One advantage, maybe a disadvantage, of motorcycles is we see and smell the changes up close. This ride demonstrated that disadvantage.

Second, humans play a significant role. Seth Borenstein with The Associated Press compiled evidence for the role of humans in his 2022 article "Climate Questions: How Do We Know Humans Triggered Warming?" Here's his conclusion:

> Over the last century or so, there's more carbon-12 in the atmosphere compared to carbon-13 and less carbon-14 in recent decades, according to NOAA. Carbon-12 is essentially fossil carbon from long ago, as in fossil fuels. So the change in the ratio of carbon-12 to carbon-13 tells scientists the carbon in the air is more from burning fossil fuels than natural carbon ... That's the fingerprint of burning coal, oil and natural gas.[1]

I encourage you to read the entire article—it persuaded me.

Third, we can do something. Back in SoCal in the '50s and '60s, our air was a foul, brown witch's brew—several of my cross country meets had to be canceled for health reasons. My college roommate from Sacramento drove into Los Angeles at night and never knew mountains surrounded the L.A. basin ... until months later when our first rainstorm drowned the smog—temporarily. But we addressed the pollution, and we can again see the mountains and breathe deeply. We can address this issue too, for God's sake. For our children's and grandchildren's sakes.

I'm not as concerned about the specifics as they can be worked out. But I suggest we who follow Jesus view this as a spiritual issue, not a financial one. Maybe short-term profit should yield to long-term creation care. While we have use of the earth, it belongs to him:

> The earth is the LORD's, and everything in it,
>   the world, and all who live in it;
> for he founded it upon the seas
>   and established it upon the waters.
> (Psalm 24:1–2)

We don't own the earth. In effect, we lease it from God and are accountable to him for how we treat it.

I still fight resentment at a management company that took poor care of our house when we rented it out for six years. They didn't carry out the contracted monthly drive-by inspections, just took the word of the landscapers, and when we first walked in after the tenants left and the management company cleared them, our wood floors had buckled from an unreported water leak. Fixing it all cost over $20,000.

How must God feel when he looks at what we've done to his earth? Pretty clear, isn't it? He gave us use of the earth. Our job is to take care of it so it can meet our needs as we honor the Giver.

KICK-STARTING THE APPLICATION

What has been your position on the reality of climate change? If you read the AP link, how did it impact you? Do you see this as a spiritual issue? Why or why not? What action will you take to help care for God's earth?

36—THE TASTE OF GRAVEL

By Pam St. Schmoll, AUTHOR, TEACHER, MISSION WORKER

I dreamed I was being chased, but I was not asleep. Pursued by a truck, brakes slamming, knocked sideways, and gravel tossed. I lived to tell the story you are reading. On my 16th birthday, my parents gave me a cedar hope chest ... and a motorcycle. My parents had hoped for a namesake but got three daughters. They planned on naming me Robert Gene. I now understand I am here because of God's wisdom—Mom had a diagnosis that may have made a rowdy house of boys quite challenging for her. I felt loved but remember the summer I spent playing pirate in the bamboo out back. By the end of that summer, the neighbor asked my mom what had happened to my eye—I had been wearing an eyepatch. All these decisions made me bold and adventurous.

Our family roots are in Colorado, and we often camped at Cedaredge up on Grand Mesa. We loaded all the motorbikes onto a trailer and towed them to the countryside for vacation fun. We had cousins, pine trees, and birds singing—heavenly. I was never a serious biker because I didn't like the exposure to danger, but I still met the challenge of the back roads with my younger sister on the back. I also regretted every mosquito bite.

That afternoon, a fast driver in a nightmare truck miscalculated and knocked us over onto the gravel. I had no major damage except for my nerves. What if my little sister had been seriously injured? Hello to the reality of other drivers and my utter lack of confidence as a biker.

A variety of similar experiences like this came along because I never felt limited by a traditional woman's role. I learned to model the strengths of both parents. Before retiring into some mission work, I had three careers. I taught high school in private and public schools, then used a degree from UCLA to work as an R & D chemist (a male-dominated field). That career sent me to Alaska to work on the pipeline. I built two successful real estate businesses in two states, then went to auctions to purchase and flip homes. Construction was my dad's career.

That motorcycle opened doors for me by making me brave. Though never a true tomboy, I did not feel limited by my femininity or experience any "ceiling." God had a design in mind when he knit me in my mother's womb. Neither my dad's wish for a son nor machines too fast for me changed the course of my life. I just returned from eight European countries, living in five and serving the Lord in three. I am so grateful for that bike, that summer, and my parents. Am I exactly "right" now? No—but I am adventurous. The motorcycle did that. Today I'm girly-girly yet have earned three speeding tickets in the last two years—driving a solid SUV.

Notice the first sentence of that last paragraph: "That motorcycle opened doors for me by making me brave." Riding changes us, and what we learn on a bike can often spill over into all facets of our lives. Cowards rarely ride or soon quit. Many choose to stop at their first drop or close call. Pam discovered bikes weren't for her, but not out of cowardness—they revealed her courage to her, courage that led to an adventurous life few of us could conceive of. She translated the bravery from biking into a character trait. How do we all build courage?

One, we ride. We face the dangers and risks and build the courage to continue. We discover our courage exceeds our fears. Another chapter explores how we only discover our limits when we push them. So we push our envelope of safety into adventure and accomplishment. But we still need more sources.

Two, we learn the tools of a task. How do we gain the courage to corner fast? We talk to experienced riders about their tricks, like counter steering, leaning, reading a corner, or setting up a line. So then we go a little bit faster than before, then once again a little faster, and finally it becomes instinctive. Only courageous fools take stupid risks they're not ready to take. This principle transcends biking and applies to almost every task.

Three, we grow courage by relying on God's presence in our lives. In the times of Joshua, the people of Israel approached the promised land, abundant but filled with giant warriors. Their earlier fear caused them to wander for four decades, but the cowards had now died, and God said, "Move in." Then he gave a special message to Joshua, their leader: "Be *strong and courageous*. Do not be afraid; do not be discouraged, for the LORD *your God will be with you wherever you go*" (Joshua 1:9). That command to be strong and brave based on God's presence was given three times in four verses. Why? They would soon learn how much power his presence brought them.

For about 10 years now, my prayers have changed when friends face death, surgery, or difficulties. I rarely ask God for a specific result. He knows better than I what is best. But I always ask that they sense his very real presence and gain comfort and courage from it and that he does his best for them.

The good news? We can use our experiences and God's presence to have the needed courage to face anything that comes our way.

Kick-Starting the Application

Do you see yourself as timid or brave? Has that changed over the years? Are you facing something now that requires bravery? How can focusing on God's presence increase your courage?

Pam St. Schmoll lives in the Pacific Northwest but was homegrown in Southern California. This sinner saved by grace enjoyed careers in teaching, chemistry, and real estate. Now retired, she has transitioned into writing and mission work. A gifted connector and communicator, Pam is famous for her sweet tooth. Visit her blog at pamschmoll.com or contact her at pam@pamschmoll.com.

37—TWO-WEEK TRIP TAKES SIX MONTHS

Only significant backstory explains how a two-week trip could take four months, so here's the scoop. Back in 2022, Jerry and I, the two remaining core members of the Gray Hogs, attempted a 17-or-so-day East Coast trip. Jerry needed to add 38 states to bag all the lower 48 on a bike—this trip would do it. I needed just three to finish all 50. We had to do some meandering to make it work and spent a lot of time examining possible routes. We figured about 10,000 miles should do it, ranging from Oregon and California to Florida to Maine and back. In our mid-70s, yes, we were ambitious.

The trip went well. In a little over a week, we traveled from our West Coast homes to the Southeast, where I bagged my last three states: Florida, Georgia, and South Carolina. Crossing into South Carolina both thrilled and relieved me.

But we had some issues—miscommunicating with each other along with some relatively minor decisions that could have backfired seriously. Then in Connecticut, 10 states short for Jerry, his Can Am Spyder died on an interstate ramp behind me, and, as I attempted to get back to him, a van and my bike collided, totaling my Goldwing. Did God perhaps not want us to finish it? I'm not sure, but I did wonder. We explored a lot of options, but I had no bike, and Jerry didn't trust his, so I rented a car to drive home to California, and Jerry flew back to Oregon.

Once back, Jerry had little desire to finish his goal in 2023. But little desire changed into openness, which grew into certainty. He helped me get my last states, so I wanted to return the favor. We made a plan for 2023. We'd leave our homes and meet in Evanston, Wyoming, then head east on I-80 and 90, do a brief dip into Rhode Island, then up to Maine, and home. Mission accomplished in two weeks. Jerry would have his 49 states, all but Alaska; he'd already picked up Hawaii on a cruise.

He planned on leaving Oregon on Friday, and I'd leave Temecula on Saturday, but he called me Friday morning feeling a lot of pain in his hip and leg. He tried it, though, and the tough little guy made it to Burley, Idaho, about 660 miles. But on that night's phone discussion, he decided to head back; he had no confidence for the long trip. Once home, he felt a little better, but not well enough to make the East Coast. He suggested a one-week ride in Oregon near his home, and we enjoyed a fine week in the Oregon backcountry and got drenched on the jet boats in Grants Pass, Oregon.

But that was just one week of riding with a two-week goal. His leg pain became manageable, and he was a bit bugged about what we missed. He came up with another idea—another week's ride in the fall, meeting in Chico, California, and exploring the back roads of the northwest California mountains. Honestly, the 20 miles east of Happy Camp gave us one of our best marriages of road, rider, and machine, as told in chapter 40.

But on the last night of this trip, his leg again acted up, so once more we cut it short. We got in the two weeks, though, in three sections in the six months from May to October. More than just the joy of riding together and completing our goal, this ride reminded me of some key spiritual truths: in riding and following, we need some goals yet flex in how we reach them.

Our key goal should be to desperately seek God: "Anyone who comes to him must believe that he exists and that he rewards those *who earnestly seek him*" (Hebrews 11:6). I've only found two categories regarding God's will for all people—that we know and grow in him. He wants a relationship with us as our Lord and Savior. Second Peter 3:9 tells us, "The Lord is ... not wanting anyone to perish, but everyone to come to repentance." Then 1 Thessalonians 4:3 tells us we need to develop godly lives: "It is God's will that *you should be sanctified*."

Those are the primary spiritual goals God has for us, and may I suggest we don't flex on these primary goals?

But he gives us a great deal of freedom in crafting our lives with his guidance. Remember Proverbs 16:9: "We can make our plans, but the LORD *determines* our steps."

Honestly, as long as our plans match knowing and growing, we have a lot of room here. I've found no biblical evidence God has planned out every step of our lives. My goal of 50 states on two wheels matches that. Well, as long as we didn't steal new Goldwings for the trip.

Paul the apostle amazes me with his life's turns. A rabid Jew who prosecuted and killed Christians changed to a rabid follower who took Jesus to most of the known world. And he also understood the freedom to make our own decisions: "Now when I went to Troas to preach the gospel of Christ and found that the Lord had opened a door for me, I still had no peace of mind, because I did not find my brother Titus there. So I said goodbye to them and went on to Macedonia" (2 Corinthians 2:12–13).

Honestly, I expected a lightning bolt to turn Paul into a crispy critter for ignoring an open door for him to do what he loved—tell people about Jesus. But look at the next verse: "But thanks be to God, who *always leads us ... in Christ's triumphal procession*" (2 Corinthians 2:14). Don't miss the significance here. God opened a door, Paul went the opposite way, and God still led in triumph.

Yes, Jerry and I adapted our plans. I think we listened to the whispers of the Spirit. May we all seek God earnestly, cling to the main goals, and flex.

KICK-STARTING THE APPLICATION

Have you grasped the freedom to flex on matters with no clear scriptural command? How do you choose to change a plan? What factors in for you—prayer, circumstances, or input from friends? How do you keep on track to know and grow in him?

38—WILL THIS EVER END

Insanity or idiocy? Or a demented desire to identify and challenge my limits? Just about all my family and friends thought the first two would explain my attempt at an Iron Butt ride: 1,000 miles on two wheels in 24 hours. I lean toward a strange blend of all three.

On the insane and idiot side, I was 70 with a bum left knee. The 4 a.m. departure time would work against a needed good night's sleep. The planned route of 1,040 miles would take about 14 hours of butt-on-seat time, with six stops for bike fuel—three including human fuel—adding maybe four hours. Eighteen hours after my 4 a.m. departure in Temecula would hopefully see me in the Motel 6 at Dillon, Montana, about 10 p.m. Well, make that 11 p.m. with the time change. One long day. Could I make it? I did one easily at 28, but that was ancient history. I had many reasons not to try it.

On the challenging limits side, my competitive streak has mostly morphed into competing with myself—determining how my limits have changed by pressing them. I yearn to live as fully and wisely as I can.

What made me think it possible? I had accomplished one already. My Honda ST1300 was set for long-distance touring with highway pegs, a driver backrest, a cup holder (to hold coffee in the morning and then ice water), and a range of 300 miles per tank. I'd ridden most of that almost-straight road before and much of it had speed limits of 75 to 80. I pulled out my maps and planned every stop. My max projected miles on any leg were 180. Just two years before, a friend and I rode 700 miles up 395 in California to Redding in 16 hours, much with rainy fog, so I'd recently ridden the same hours.

But most importantly, completing the Iron Butt wasn't my main goal—that was to arrive alive at wherever the day ended. Giving my wife that assurance and using the Redding ride as an example helped her to accede.

The stop at Cedar City, Utah, was nearly the halfway point, 465 miles. I arrived by 10:30 a.m., well ahead of schedule. But already sore and tired, I took a good break until noon. I'd begun to notice that MapQuest's predicted distances didn't match reality. The leg to Brigham City featured both some rain and traffic, with 300 miles to go—a very long 300 miles for a tired 70-year-old. So, I required a longer and unplanned rest in some version of a 7-11 with hard plastic seats.

I needed another longer break at Idaho Falls before hitting the last stretch to Dillon. By then I realized MapQuest missed it by 40 miles, making the total now 1,080. My spirits plummeted—more time on that granite seat. I truly wondered if it would ever end. The bike loved to fly, so we kept up with Idaho and Montana traffic, which helped. Barely. Finally, at 9:40 local time, 16.3 hours after first hitting the start switch, I turned the bike off for the last time that day. Mission Impossible became Mission Accomplished. A very tough day.

We all face difficulties that seem to have no end point in sight. Cancer. Relationships. Jobs. Pain. Depression. And we wonder if we can get through. Discouragement grows, and we're ready to give up. We feel much like I felt like in Idaho Falls—beat, with too many miles left. The biblical word *patience*, part of the fruit of the Spirit, literally means *long-suffering*. So, how do we respond when suffering goes on longer than we desire?

The first Iron Butt lesson encourages us to determine when the difficulty might end, if we can gauge it. Some hard times "come to pass, not to stay." Knowing they're temporary can bring us some hope. Others won't conclude, so we need to come to grips and think long-term.

Frankly, sometimes a problem never ends in this life. Followers of Jesus die from cancer. Divorce ends the dreams of a lifetime. Sometimes the ultimate healing and relief only comes as we enter heaven. And with still more others, we have no clue if it's temporary or forever, so maybe we benefit by playing the long game.

A second lesson comes with crafting some tools that help us arrive at our heavenly destination. For the first step, copy what I learned in Idaho Falls: stop and rest. The rest revived me enough to hop on the Honda and finish. Let me suggest when we face troubles with an uncertain ending, we find ways to revive ourselves, physically and emotionally and mentally and spiritually. Yes, the method will vary for each of us. We need to know ourselves. That can keep us going and give us the best chance to outrun the hard times.

Third, how do we face any suffering and finish our course? We rely on what will never run out:

The faithful love of the Lord never ends!

> His mercies never cease.
> Great is his faithfulness;
>   his mercies begin afresh each morning.
> (Lamentations 3:22–23 NLT)

God's love and presence never end. His supply of mercy gets refilled every day.

We can focus on his presence in our lives, every second of every day. We remind ourselves he loves us. He wants our best and works in all things. I can't understand all God does or why. But I rely on the truth he loves us and works with us in all things. He will help us arrive alive ... in heaven.

KICK-STARTING THE APPLICATION

Have you had some problems in the past you thought would never end, yet did? How did you handle them? How deeply did you involve God in them? Do you have some current difficulties that have extended beyond your deadline? What tools to revive you are available? How does the assurance of God's love help you in the pain?

39—LONGING FOR BELONGING

By Cherie Denna, *author, speaker, biker*

The abrupt end of my 17-year marriage sent my world spinning. My faith, once a vibrant fire, now struggled to burn amid the relentless invasion of PTSD triggers. Despite the dangers of the online social scene, I navigated through chat groups to reconnect with the biker world. Returning to the outlaw biker clubs stirred up a nostalgic longing for the sense of belonging I'd carried since my early childhood.

Memorial Day weekend offered ample opportunities for riding, but one event stood out. The Memorial Day ride, the mother of all rallies, drew chapters of the Vietnam Vets Motorcycle Club (VNVMC) from across the nation. A sea of red and black leather enveloped the local campground. The highlight of the evening? Witnessing a group of burly prospects belt out "Stand by Your Man" around the bonfire. After getting acquainted with a few wives of the club brothers, I received an invitation to join the VNVMC on their ride to the California Vietnam Veterans Memorial.

The next morning, I took my place at the rear of the over 200-bike pack. We rode in formation along the highway, proudly flying the American and POW flags. Cars shifted lanes, honking their horns in solidarity. A profound sense of reverence and honor welled up within me for these warriors.

The solemnity of the Memorial Day ceremony at the Vietnam Veterans Memorial hung heavy in the air. Veterans and their families searched the memorial wall to locate the names of the fallen. Compassion and sorrow gripped my heart. I longed to remain among them. *I'll prove myself worthy. I found my people.* Not outlaws, but activists and advocates who stood for something honorable. They were all heroes in my book.

The following month, one of the VNVMC officers invited me to ride with him to a private event hosted by another club. Though I set up my own camp spot, my chaperone escorted me to the VNVMC camp. Whenever I approached their campfire, I couldn't help but question if the club president considered me worthy of the esteemed "property patch," a patch exclusively worn by a fully patched club member's ole lady. This mindset led me to sacrifice pieces of myself at the altar of belonging.

Despite my wavering heart, I discerned gentle nudges urging me to turn to Jesus. He compelled me to openly express my faith to the bikers I rode alongside.

During my quest for belonging, God intervened. He helped me see how the enemy lured and ensnared me into those camps by creating the illusion of a safe and secure environment. I endured intense bouts of spiritual warfare. The devil spewed lies about my self-worth, but I continued to cry out to the Lord, and he rescued my prodigal spirit.

Following years of healing and recovery, I encountered a deeper, more intimate understanding of my belovedness in Christ. He protected me while among the lost in preparation for future ministry. I thank God for his merciful and unwavering love, entrusting me to guide the outcasts on their journey toward true belonging.

MORE GOD, MOTORCYCLES, AND OPEN ROAD | 157

Cherie's story reminds me of the old Johnny Lee song "Lookin' for Love" where he ends up finding "love" in places he shouldn't. We humans have deep-seated needs for belonging with others, loving relationships, significance in our lives, provision for our needs, and transcendence beyond ourselves. Fully aware of them, Satan entices us with counterfeit methods to meet them.

Those alternatives come with two problems. First, they can't meet the deepest hungers of our souls. Cherie discovered that truth, as did I. After growing up in church, I began to question everything in college, which led me on a four-year spiritual search. When in grad school as a grad assistant, on the surface, life was great. Living in off-campus housing with a rarely present friend, a cool car and motorcycle, three irregular girlfriends, straight A's. Life couldn't get any better. But like Cherie found, a good life didn't satisfy the hunger of my soul. My lifestyle couldn't change some basic character flaws. God did.

Second, counterfeits lead us away from God. We find alternatives to him—what society, friends, family, and our sinful inner tendencies tell us to seek out. We say times have changed or we want to be on the "right side of history." We yearn to fit in. We doubt God knows best. And so we look outside of God to deeply feed our souls.

Why do the alternatives not work? Very simply, God does know us best, what our deepest needs are, and how to meet them. He created us. He loves us. He wants the best for us. Listen to Jesus's goals for us: "I came so they can have real and eternal life, more and better life than they ever dreamed of" (John 10:10 MSG).

My searching had two flaws. I thought meeting my needs was all up to me. And when it gets down to it, I thought

I knew better than God how my life should be lived. Oh, he gives us that option, but it comes with a high cost. Dissatisfaction. I've learned I truly can rely on God to work in all the dimensions of my life for good: "And my God will meet all your needs according to the riches of his glory in Christ Jesus" (Philippians 4:19).

Kris Kristofferson gave the key in his song "To Beat the Devil." As a discouraged singer, tempted to give up, he knew he had to remain true to his soul's hunger. He found the only way to do that was the title to his song, to beat the devil. Beating the devil meant saying no to counterfeit solutions and embracing God's ways.

KICK-STARTING THE APPLICATION

How often have you fallen for counterfeit solutions to your deepest soul needs? How did those work out for you? For you, what works best in seeking God's path? Is there a verse you can rely on to help you stay on track?

Cherie Denna's mission is to empower individuals to find a deep sense of belonging and belovedness in Jesus Christ. Cherie influences the world through writing, speaking, and women's ministry. You can join the Everyday Belonging Movement at www.cheriedenna.com or order Cherie's debut book, *Beloved Outcast: The Quest for True Belonging* at https://a.co/d/1iCdJao.

40—MAN, MACHINE, MACADAM

This story happened on what I term "The Last Ride" in September 2023, after our aborted May attempt to finish Jerry's 49 states on a bike. The pain from a bad case of sciatica ended the plan for a 17-day ride the first day, but we did get in one week in Oregon. Yet we both desired more riding, so we met in Chico, California, for a week in the mountains and coastal roads of northwest California.

Beyond riding, Jerry wanted to see if his 76-year-old body could continue to enjoy long rides. Would this be the last? Would we continue the long rides we loved? This trip would give us a clue.

The trip began awkwardly for me, since my 2014 Honda CTX1300 was still new, with only that medium-length ride in Oregon. This was one tired biker the first night in Santa Nella. The next day's putt to Chico didn't hurt as much, but handling this bike hadn't yet become instinctive.

From Chico, we wound through back roads up to Yreka, and I felt the bike and me coming back into harmony. Not full, but closer. I smiled a lot on the back roads yet had no clue of the joy to come the next day.

The first 75 miles west on Highway 96 followed the Klamath River on a two-lane road, and the vistas intrigued me. A few curves brought some challenge but not much. The bike and I were getting accustomed to each other, and the difference in handling the tighter turns compared to my previous Goldwing pleased me.

A small and funky café in Happy Camp with two unique older servers provided good sandwiches and a very fine beer. Then we headed west, intending to spend the night at the Blue Lake Casino/Hotel, a little northeast of Eureka, a good stop if you're in the area. Then came one of those God moments, a grace surprise.

As we left Happy Camp, the road changed to 30 miles of gently linked curves, each with their consistent radius. I set the speed and angle of lean at the start of a curve and made no adjustments until the next curve approached. The road had very few straight sections, just curve after curve after curve.

Lean left, hold it, then swing over to leaning right. Wash, rinse, dry, repeat. With no traffic to slow us down, we went at a pleasing but not crazy speed, with a marvelous and rare rhythm. Thirty miles of sensing the oneness of the rider, the road, the bike. All three worked together for joy and worship and ecstasy. A nice trinity of man, machine, and macadam. Then the thought hit me.

That road gave me an insight into a metaphor of a far greater trinity—the Father, Son, and Holy Spirit. So, let's explore a very brief description of the Trinity, then how the Trinity gives us a fine ride through life. We finite beings cannot fully comprehend how three persons can be one, but we do know they were all divine. Just look at Genesis 1:1–2 to see how the Father and Spirit were divine agents of creation, and then at John 17:5 to see Jesus was there with the other two: "Father, glorify me in your presence with the glory I had with you *before the world began.*"

Three persons, yet one. Deuteronomy 6:4 says, "Hear, O Israel: The Lord our God, *the Lord is one.*" A helpful metaphor, although imperfect, is an egg. Each of the three parts, the shell, the white, and the yolk, are all and only egg. Yet none are the entire egg. Okay, that's the end of looking at God's nature in three persons, so let's do a quick flyby of how all three persons work together to enrich our lives.

- *All save us.* They're each part of the salvation process, as we see in Matthew 28:19: "Therefore go and make disciples of all nations, baptizing them in the name of the *Father and of the Son and of the Holy Spirit*" (Matthew 28:19). The start of our spiritual life flows from the Trinity.

- *All unite us.* Paul encourages us to "Make every effort to keep the unity of the Spirit through the bond of peace" in Ephesians 4:3. Then he gives seven sources of unity, including the one Spirit, one Lord (Jesus), and one God and Father. Sharing each person in the Trinity allows us to transcend our differences and become one ourselves.

- *All share glory among themselves and with us.* Clearly, the Creator has glory, or splendor, as does Jesus: "Father, glorify me in your presence with the glory I had with you before the world began" (John 17:5). But—and here's the exciting stuff—they share that glory with us: "So all of us who have had that veil removed can see and *reflect* the glory of the Lord. And the Lord—who is the Spirit—makes us *more and more like him as we are changed into his glorious image*" (2 Corinthians 3:18 NLT). Have you noticed that glow that some Christians have? Thank the Trinity.

- *All teach us.* All that Jesus taught came from the Father, and then the Spirit teaches it to us: "These words you hear are not my own; they belong to the Father who sent me ... the Advocate, the Holy Spirit, whom the Father will send in my name, will teach you all things" (John 14:24, 26). Pretty authoritative stuff!

- *All live in us.* Seeing how the omniscient Father is in us, according to Ephesians 4:6 (NLT), amazes me: "one God and Father, who is over all and in all and living through all." Jesus and the Holy Spirit are also in us. Jesus says in Matthew 28:20, "And surely I am with you always," and John 14:17 tell us, "The Spirit ... lives with you and will be in you."

As nice as that combo of man, machine, and macadam was, the Trinity beats it.

PS—As I first wrote this in March 2024, Jerry couldn't sell his bike, and his leg improved, so in May of 2024 we took an 11-day ride to Nevada, Arizona, Utah, and Idaho ... so who knows for 2025?

Kick-Starting the Application

Have you thought much before about the practical dimensions of the Trinity? Have you neglected one? Maybe spend some time reading those passages and ponder how the Trinity can enrich your walk.

A NOTE FROM THE AUTHOR

I hope and pray *More God, Motorcycles, and Open Roads* challenged you—to ride more, to love God more, to understand bikers more, to serve more, to grow more in him. This book gives a great metaphor about all our journeys with Jesus, whether we ride or not. Looking for the "small" events shows how we can better see him in the everyday.

So, let's keep this going. I love to connect with my readers. My blog, *Unconventional*, at timriter.com has a fresh post each week about weaving faith into the fabric of our lives. You can find a lot of bike stories there.

Feel free to friend me on Facebook. I post often about my bike trips.

I also do some speaking, having spent decades as a pastor and university professor. If you need a speaker for a conference, men's group, or any type of event, just get in touch with me at timriter@aol.com.

Now let's close this adventure as we began, with Psalm 45:3–4 (MSG):

> Ride majestically! Ride triumphantly!
> Ride on the side of truth!
> Ride for the righteous meek!"

And ride safely!

ABOUT THE AUTHOR

Starting with no interest at all in bikes, enduring a neighbor's insistence to try his kid's Honda Trail 90, then being intrigued with the classic film *Easy Rider*, Tim Riter has grown to embrace motorcycles. He's totaled 270,000 miles riding, encompassing all 50 states, plus Washington, DC, Canada, and Mexico. The unity of rider, road, and bike has given him a unique perspective on God's creation, revealing glimpses of God in some unusual situations.

Tim spent over 20 years as a pastor. His years in ministry, combined with equal time in education, from junior high to high school to university, and teaching science, communication, and composition, all contribute to his 30 years as an author. His writing spans Christian-living nonfiction, two motorcycle devotional books, and even a book of poetry, for a total of twelve books (with more on tap). A few of his poems are sprinkled in this book.

In addition to pastoring, writing, and teaching, Tim has enjoyed a variety of other careers. He was a caretaker for an unused guest ranch in the mountains above Taos and worked in hotel management, in quality control at a company making parts for the space shuttle, as a real estate broker, and more. He and his wife, Sheila, live in the Old West town of Temecula in SoCal, where they love trips to the beaches and mountains and traveling all over the West.

ENDNOTES

Chapter Two
1. *Merriam-Webster.com Dictionary*, s.v. "wild," accessed July 6, 2024, https://www.merriam-webster.com/dictionary/wild.

Chapter Seven
Harold Kushner, When Bad Things Happen to Good People (Palatine, IL: Anchor, 2004).

Chapter Twelve
1. Matthew P. White et al., "Spending at Least 120 Minutes a Week in Nature Is Associated with Good Health and Wellbeing," *Scientific Reports* 9, 7730 (2019): https://doi.org/10.1038/s41598-019-44097-3.

2. Andrew Cherney, "New Study Finds Motorcycle Riding Decreases Stress, Increases Focus," Cycle World, January 18, 2019, https://www.cycleworld.com/new-study-finds-motorcycle-riding-decreases-stress-increases-focus/.

Chapter Twenty-One
1. To learn more on how to espalier trees, visit https://www.bhg.com/gardening/trees-shrubs-vines/care/how-to-espalier/.

Chapter Twenty-Two
1. Johanna McFarland, "Why Are Deserts so Good?," NCESC.com, June 21, 2024, https://www.ncesc.com/geographic-faq/why-are-deserts-so-good/.

2. Grammenos Mastrojeni, "Why Mountains Matter," One Earth, November 30, 2023, https://www.oneearth.org/why-mountains-matter/.

Chapter Twenty-Six

1. Paula Peterson, "Father and Son Accused of Starting Caldor Fire Won't Stand Trial Due to Lack of Evidence," South Tahoe Now, January 8, 2024, https://www.southtahoenow.com/story/01/08/2024/father-and-son-accused-starting-caldor-fire-wont-stand-trial-due-lack-evidence.

2. Sophie Reardon, "PG&E Electrical Equipment Sparked Massive Dixie Fire in California, Investigation Finds," CBS News, January 5, 2022, https://www.cbsnews.com/news/pacific-gas-and-electric-company-cause-dixie-fire-california/.

3. Antoinette Radford et al., "January 9, 2024—Winter Storm Slams Central and Eastern US," CNN, January 10, 2024, https://www.cnn.com/us/live-news/eastern-us-snow-storm-01-09-24/index.html.

4. *Merriam-Webster.com Legal Dictionary*, s.v. "fiduciary relationship," accessed August 8, 2024, https://www.merriam-webster.com/legal/fiduciary%20relationship.

Chapter Thirty-Three

1. Olivia Guy-Evans, "The Psychology of Fear: Definition, Symptoms, Traits, Causes, Treatment," Simply Psychology, July 20, 2023, https://www.simplypsychology.org/what-is-fear.html.

Chapter Thirty-Five

1. Seth Borenstein, "Climate Questions: How Do We Know Humans Triggered Warming?," AP News, November 6, 2022, https://apnews.com/article/science-climate-and-environment-099266b36d6e637d405dead6f0914a0f.

www.ingramcontent.com/pod-product-compliance
Lightning Source LLC
Chambersburg PA
CBHW060656100426
42734CB00047B/1943